CANADIAN CURRENTS

Patricia M. Singh

Patricia A. Morrison

Oxford University Press
1995

Oxford University Press Canada
70 Wynford Drive Don Mills Ontario M3C 1J9

Oxford New York
Athens Auckland Bangkok Bombay
Calcutta Cape Town Dar es Salaam Delhi
Florence Hong Kong Istanbul Karachi
Kuala Lumpur Madras Madrid Melbourne
Mexico City Nairobi Paris Singapore
Tapei Tokyo Toronto

and associated companies in
Berlin Ibadan

This book is printed on permanent (acid-free) paper.

Canadian Cataloguing in Publication Data

Morrison, Patricia A., 1949-   .
Canadian currents: an activity-based grammar
for new canadians

ISBN 0-19-541060-2

1. English language - Textbooks for second language
learners.* 2. English language - Grammar -
Problems, exercises, etc. I. Singh, Patricia M.,
1956- . II. Title

PE1128.M67 1995   428.2'4   C94-932456-6

Editors: Robert Doyle, Mary Lindsey
Editorial Assistant: Micaëla Gates
Design: Heather Delfino
Layout: McGraphics Desktop Publishing Ltd.
Illustrations: Mark Thurman, Janet Wilson
Cover design: Opus House

Printed and bound in Canada by The Bryant Press

1 2 3 4 5 99 98 97 96 95

Acknowledgements

The publisher and authors wish to thank the following people for their contributions in reviewing the manuscript for this text:

Suzanne Murdock, Community Language Services, Language Studies Canada

The Sanderson Library Intermediate class and those colleagues who field tested many of these ideas and activities.

The authors would also like to extend their gratitude to their friends and family for their patience and support. Special thanks to Robert Doyle for his significant contribution to this project.

About the Authors

PATRICIA M. SINGH has an honours degree in Modern Languages from the University of Toronto. She also has a diploma from the Sociedad Mangold in Spain as well as a certificate from the Paris Chamber of Commerce. She has completed a certificate course in TESL offered by the Ministry of Citizenship and Culture. During the course of her eleven-year career in ESL, Ms. Singh has developed ESL curriculum and examinations. She was a member of the Steering Committee charged with establishing ESL teaching standards in Ontario community colleges. Ms. Singh is currently Director of Studies at a private language school in Toronto and is actively involved in the training of teachers of ESL.

PATRICIA A. MORRISON has a degree in Speech Arts and Drama from the Royal Conservatory in Toronto, a degree in Psychology, specializing in Linguistics and Language Acquisition and a degree in TESL from McGill University in Montreal, and a postgraduate degree in Applied Linguistics and Multicultural Education from the Ontario Institute for Studies in Education. She has taught ESL at the University of Quebec at Montreal and at Sir Sanford Fleming College in Peterborough. Ms. Morrison is currently teaching for the Toronto Board of Education.

Photo Credits

11 Canapress (John Felstead); 18 (1) Andrew Vaughan/Canapress; (2) Joy Kogawa; (3) Frank Gunn/Canapress; (4) Frank Gunn/Canapress; (5) Ron Poling/Canapress; (6) Graeme Gibson; (7) Jacques Boissinot/Canapress; (8) Felstead/Canapress; (9) Remiorz/Canapress; 29 (1) National Archives of Canada; (2) Canapress H/O; (4) Canapress H/O; (5) Canapress (P. Chiasson); 59 Ian Douglas; 78 St. John Ambulance Saint-Jean; 93 The Law Courts Education Society of B.C.; 127 The Ontario Lacrosse Association; 142 West Edmonton Mall; 157 Sue Brun/Canapress; 158 (l & r) Dave Buston/Canapress; 159 Dave Buston/Canapress; 161 National Archives of Canada/C29459; 171 (t) National Archives of Canada/C3693; (r) National Archives of Canada/C6512; (m) Saskatchewan Archives Board/R-A2294; (b) National Archives of Canada/D-36-15; 192 Provincial Archives of Alberta/E. Brown Collection/B 6022

Contents

To the Teacher
Page vi

	Themes	Functions and Themes	Grammar
Unit 1 Page 1	A Fresh Start	– talking about work and workday routines – describing ourselves and others	– review of simple present, present continuous – adverbs of frequency
Unit 2 Page 21	Job Hunting	– talking about past experiences and achievements – exploring job hunting strategies – refining job hunting skills – preparing cover letters and resumes	– review of simple past and present perfect – time expressions: <u>since</u>, <u>for</u>, <u>already</u>, <u>yet</u>, <u>just</u>, <u>before</u>, <u>after</u>
Unit 3 Page 47	Keeping Healthy	– talking about health and medical services – making suggestions, giving advice – asking about insurance and prescriptions, regulations and policies	– modals with present and future meanings
Unit 4 Page 63	Safety First	– dealing with medical emergencies – talking about safety regulations and procedures – reporting accidents and injuries	– modals with past meanings – indirect speech
Unit 5 Page 81	Moving Ahead	– making future plans – talking about educational opportunities	– simple future tense – future intention with <u>be going to</u> – present tenses with future meaning – first conditional (future possible)

Unit 6 Page 95	**A Place of Our Own**	– finding a place to live – making comparisons – talking about housing issues and concerns	– comparative with <u>er</u> – comparative with <u>more...than</u>, <u>less...than</u> – superlative with <u>the...est</u> – superlative with <u>the most...</u> – progressive trends with <u>more and more</u>
Unit 7 Page 113	**Just for Fun**	– discussing activities, hobbies, leisure, and recreational pursuits – describing feelings, interests, and attitudes	– gerunds and infinitives
Unit 8 Page 131	**Shopping Around**	– talking about consumer concerns and consumer services	– non-separable and separable phrasal verbs
Unit 9 Page 145	**Going Places**	– making travel plans and arrangements	– perfect modals – second conditional (present unreal)
Unit 10 Page 163	**Taking Part**	– preparing for citizenship – discussing past actions – discussing political participation – rights and freedoms	– past perfect, past perfect continuous – third conditional (past unreal) – indirect speech
Unit 11 Page 179	**Reasons to Celebrate**	– talking about customs, traditions, holidays, and festivals – discussing history	– passive voice – <u>used to</u> and <u>would</u> – past participles as adjectives – present participles as adjectives

Verb List
Page 195

To the Teacher

Canadian Currents is an intermediate level ESL text that integrates a competency based approach with a systematic grammar presentation. It is designed for adults and young adult learners who are progressing through adult education and continuing education programs across Canada. These adult learners have diverse linguistic and cultural backgrounds, education levels, learning styles, occupational histories, and hopes for a successful future in Canadian society. *Canadian Currents* is thematically organized and provides a wide variety of communicative exercises and activities to help new Canadians function more fully in their day-to-day lives.

Organization of the Text

Each unit of *Canadian Currents* is made up of four principal skill areas: **Setting the Scene, Let's Focus, Practice,** and **Work Together**. Many of the units also contain follow-up discussion topics, role plays, puzzles, games, writing exercises, questionnaires and surveys, and information gap activities using the grammar and competencies covered in the unit.

Setting the Scene serves as a warm-up and gives students an opportunity to look at the picture or illustration and to predict what is most likely going to occur in the dialogue. Setting the Scene also enables teachers to elicit key and useful vocabulary the learners may encounter. A suggested technique is to have learners describe the illustration, then ask them to speculate on what is happening. Learners may then read the dialogue and answer the questions in pairs or small groups.

Let's Focus presents the grammar structures that are first encountered in the dialogues. You may wish to have your learners isolate the structures in the dialogue and discuss their uses before exploring them in greater detail in Let's Focus. The grammatical structures are presented in a straightforward manner, using vocabulary that is readily understood by intermediate and pre-intermediate learners. Examples are provided so the learners can confirm their understanding. You may wish to have students provide more examples on their own. Although the Let's Focus sections have been presented in simple English, it is always advisable for the instructor to review the material presented before going into class. It would be better for students to have their books closed during the presentation of Let's Focus. This would allow students to concentrate more on the oral explanation and to use the text presentation as a reference or resource.

Practice exercises are designed to provide graded and controlled practice of the material presented in Let's Focus. Depending on the needs of your classes, the material in each Practice may be used for oral exercises or as written tasks. We would recommend, however, that the learners be encouraged to approach the material as oral pair work before proceeding to individual written assignments.

Work Together situations give learners an opportunity to practise the grammatical structures in a discussion format. These assignments often involve the learners referring to authentic material and documents in order for them to make informed choices. In order to make these assignments more relevant, learners are asked to use material obtained from their own community organizations or to use material you have obtained for them. This ensures that learners are using up-to-date, topical information. Work Together includes a wide variety of exercises such as completing information gaps, conducting surveys, completing questionnaires and an accident report, discussing topical issues, planning a course of study, and designing a home.

Optional Components of Each Unit

There are a variety of Canadian content readings, activities, and role plays that you may choose to work with in class.

Let's Get Set introduces students to Canadian content readings which may be assigned as homework and followed up in class. If you choose to do the readings in class, we recommend that you put learners in groups to read silently and then ask them to answer the comprehension questions. As you monitor the groups, encourage the learners to use each other as resources when discussing vocabulary. These readings also serve as points of departure for group discussion.

Activities have been designed to allow the learners to have fun with the language. They range in complexity from simple fill-in-the-blanks exercises to more involved surveys. You may wish to assign some of the activities for homework or have learners work on them in pairs or small groups in class.

Role Play situations are those in which the learners may find themselves in real life. If you wish, you may ask students to develop their own role-play situations. In all the role-playing activities, encourage students to use the new vocabulary learned in the unit.

Glossary is found at the end of each unit. It contains new vocabulary introduced in opening dialogues, practices, and readings.

SETTING THE SCENE

1. Where are these people?

2. What is happening?

Belita:	Carla, this is Meena, our new roommate.
Carla:	Hi, Meena. I hope you'll like it here.
Meena:	Hi, Carla. I'm sure I will.
Belita:	You can put your bags in this room.
Carla:	Would you like some coffee?

Meena: Thanks, I'd love a cup.

Meena: Mmm, this coffee is good.

Belita: We always make a fresh pot when we get home.

Carla: We need it to help us *unwind* after a hard day at work.

Meena: What do you do Carla?

Carla: I'm an *admin assistant (AA)*. I work for a small company that designs computer software. It's not very exciting, but it's a steady job with regular hours. What do you do, Meena?

Meena: I'm a bank teller, but I'm thinking of going into my own business someday. In fact, I'm taking an evening course on starting a small business.

Belita: Really! That's very interesting. What kind of business?

Meena: I want to go into the import/export business. The bank is a nice place to work and it has very good *benefits*, but I want to travel and see more of the world.

Comprehension Check

1. What is the relationship of the three young women?
2. What does Carla do?
3. What does Meena do?
4. What is Meena doing in the evenings? Why?

LET'S FOCUS

PRESENT TENSE OF BE

We use the present tense of the verb <u>be</u> when we state facts or describe people, things, and emotions.

Affirmative Statements	Negative Statements	Contractions
I <u>am</u> busy.	I <u>am</u> <u>not</u> busy.	I'<u>m</u> not busy.
He She <u>is</u> busy. It	He She <u>is</u> <u>not</u> busy. It	He She'<u>s</u> busy. It
You We <u>are</u> busy. They	You We <u>are</u> <u>not</u> busy. They	You We'<u>re not</u> busy. They

Yes/No Questions

<u>Is</u> she busy?
<u>Are</u> you busy?

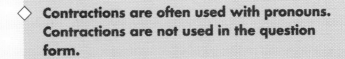

◇ **Contractions are often used with pronouns. Contractions are not used in the question form.**

◇ **We form negative contractions in the two following ways.**

1. **He'<u>s</u> <u>not</u> busy.**
2. **He <u>isn't</u> busy.**

PRACTICE 1

Complete the following with the present tense of the verb <u>be</u>.
Use contractions where possible.

Meena: What _____ your occupation, Andrea?

Andrea: I____ a salesperson in a small boutique.

Meena: _____it interesting work?

Andrea: Sometimes, but usually it_____ boring, because there _____ seldom any customers. A lot of people *browse* around but not too many actually buy anything.

Meena: _____ the people you meet nice?

Andrea: The regular customers, like Mrs. Gomez and Mrs. Simpson, ____ very nice. They ____ always pleasant.

Meena: You ____ lucky! At least it ____ quiet. At the bank it ____ usually very <u>hectic</u>, ^{very busy} especially when the computers ____ *on the blink* and that____ usually during *peak hours*. The ^{broken} _{not working} customers ____ often impatient because the lines ____ so long. These days, everyone ____ *in a rush*.

Andrea: Your job ____ too hectic and mine ____ too quiet. Well, Meena, you and I ____ *in the same boat.*

LET'S FOCUS

ADVERBS OF FREQUENCY

We use the adverbs of frequency with the simple present to indicate how often we do things.

Always	all of the time
Usually	most of the time
Frequently	much of the time
Sometimes	some of the time
Seldom	almost none of the time
Rarely	almost none of the time
Never	none of the time

Adverbs of frequency follow the verb <u>be</u> and come before main verbs. The adverb <u>sometimes</u> can come before or follow the main verb.

E X A M P L E :

It <u>seldom</u> snows in Vancouver.
It is <u>usually</u> hot in Toronto in the summer.

PRACTICE 2

Rewrite the following sentences. Replace the underlined words with an adverb of frequency.

EXAMPLE: **Carla goes to work on time <u>everyday</u>.**
                 Carla <u>always</u> goes to work on time.

1. Andrea works alone <u>most of the time</u>.

2. Belita <u>almost never</u> works in the daytime.

3. Meena works late <u>much of the time</u>.

4. Carla <u>doesn't ever</u> work overtime.

5. Belita works on weekends <u>some of the time</u>.

PRACTICE 3

Complete the answers to the following questions using the adverbs of frequency.

EXAMPLE: **Is it quiet at the bank?**
                 No, it's <u>usually</u> hectic.

1. Is Carla ever late for work? No, she's <u>n</u>_____.

2. Does Belita ever wear a uniform to work? Yes, she <u>a</u>_____.

3. Do Carla and Meena work with a computer? Yes, they <u>u</u>_____.

4. Does Carla often wear jeans to work? No, she <u>r</u>_____.

5. Is Andrea often busy at work? No, she's <u>s</u>_____.

PRACTICE 4

Use an adverb of frequency to restate these sentences. Keep the original meaning.

EXAMPLE: **Paul usually eats lunch at his desk.**
(seldom/ in a restaurant)
Paul seldom eats lunch in a restaurant.

1. Carla never does a bad job. (always/good)

2. Meena is seldom late for work. (usually/early)

3. Andrea is always courteous to the customers. (never/ rude)

4. Belita rarely leaves work early. (often/late)

5. Juanita is usually patient with her students. (rarely/ impatient)

WORK TOGETHER

Are You a Workaholic?

Many people choose to work very long hours and think their career is the most important thing in life. These people are called *workaholics*.

Using the adverbs of frequency, complete the following survey about your partner's work day.

1. Do you ever work overtime?
2. Do you ever supervise?
3. Do you ever arrange meetings?
4. Do you ever train others?
5. How often do you take additional training courses?
6. How often do you socialize with your co-workers?
7. Do you complete all your tasks on schedule?

WORK TOGETHER

8. How often do you meet with your supervisor? 1

9. How often do you solve problems at work? 4

10. Do you ever make suggestions at work? 5

11. How often do you do tasks that are not on your job description? X

12. Do you ever take work home with you? 5

13. How often do you feel you are the only one who can do the job right? 5

14. How often do you do a task yourself rather than delegate? 1

15. How often do you begin work early? 1

GIVE

5 points for each, "Always"

4 points for each, "Usually"

3 points for each, "Frequently"

2 points for each, "Sometimes"

1 point for each, "Never", "Rarely" or "Seldom"

SCORE:

60-75	<u>Workaholic:</u>	You are obsessed with work.
45-60	<u>Hardworking:</u>	You are very ambitious.
30-45	<u>Good worker:</u>	You have a healthy attitude towards work.
15-30	<u>In a rut:</u>	You're becoming bored with work.
0-15	<u>Burnt out:</u>	You should consider a career change.

WORK TOGETHER

Compare the results of the above survey with your classmates' results and discuss.

Do you have a high or a low score?
Are you surprised at the results?
Are many people in the class workaholics?

LET'S FOCUS

PRESENT TENSE

We use the simple present when we state facts; talk about routines and habits; or describe feelings and emotions.

Remember we add <u>s</u> to the verb for the 3rd person singular (he, she, it).

E X A M P L E :   **Andrea work<u>s</u> in a store.**
She sell<u>s</u> clothes.

Affirmative Statements

I
We   <u>provide</u> services to New Canadians.
You
They

He
She   <u>provides</u> services to new Canadians.
It

Negative Statements

You   <u>do not (don't) sell</u> radios.

She   <u>does not (doesn't) sell</u> radios.

Yes/No Questions

<u>Do</u> you <u>start</u> at the same time everyday?

<u>Does</u> he <u>start</u> at the same time everyday?

1. **We add <u>es</u> to verbs ending in <u>sh</u>, <u>ch</u>, <u>ss</u>, <u>o</u>**

2. **If a word ends with a consonant and <u>y</u>, we change the <u>y</u> to <u>i</u> and add <u>es</u>.**

PRACTICE 5

Complete the sentences with the correct form of the verb in parentheses.

Carla is an administrative assistant. She _____ (work) directly with the owner of the company. Her boss, Mr. Johnson, is very hardworking. Some people even_____ (call) him a *workaholic*. He usually _____ (arrive) before his staff and _____ (stay) very late. When Carla _____ (get) to work in the morning she _____ (take) her notepad and _____ (go) into Mr. Johnson's office. They _____ (meet) for about 30 minutes. Mr. Johnson and Carla _____ (discuss) the day's *priorities*. After the meeting, Carla and Mr. Johnson _____ (start) work. Carla _____ (try) to finish all her work before she _____ (leave). She _____ (like) to be busy. When she's not busy she _____ (watch) the clock all day.

PRACTICE 6

What do the following people do? Use a verb from the list below to complete the sentences.

investigate, diagnose, advise, fill, serve, cut, greet, prescribe, treat, design, style, take orders, answer

1. Doctors _____ and _____ illnesses and injuries. They also _____ medication.
2. A barber _____ and _____ men's hair.
3. Computer programmers _____ computer programs.
4. Receptionists _____ people and _____ the phone.
5. The police _____ crimes.
6. A pharmacist _____ prescriptions.
7. Stockbrokers _____ clients about investments.
8. A waiter _____ and _____ food in restaurants.

WORK TOGETHER

Work with a partner. Think of an occupation (not your own). Don't tell your partner what it is. Take turns asking each other yes/no questions until you guess the occupation.

EXAMPLE:

Student A: Do you wear a uniform?

Student B: No, I don't.

WORK TOGETHER

Find out about your partner's job or school. Ask questions about the following:

1. occupation or studies
2. company or school
3. duties
4. boss or teacher
5. colleagues or classmates
6. likes and dislikes.

WRITE ABOUT YOURSELF

What are your duties at work or school?

Do you do the same things everyday?

Write a short paragraph about your daily work or school routine.

Canada Employment Centres

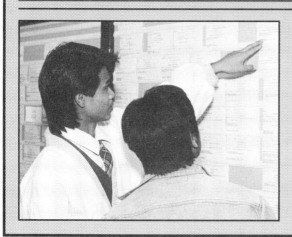

Canada Employment Centres (CEC) offer many services to job seekers. One service is a bulletin board with postings of jobs in the area. Another service is the brochure, *How to find a job*. A third service is counselling. CEC counsellors help people make career decisions, choose appropriate training and give *tips* to people seeking employment. Unemployed people register at CEC for Unemployment Insurance benefits (UI). UI provides a temporary income to unemployed people who *qualify* for these benefits.

DISCUSS ◆◆◆◆◆◆◆◆◆◆◆◆◆◆◆◆◆◆◆◆◆◆◆

1. Do you know of any other CEC services?
2. Does your country of origin offer similar services?

LET'S FOCUS

PRESENT CONTINUOUS

We use the present continuous tense of the verb when we talk about actions that are in progress; actions that began in the past and are still in progress; actions that will occur in the immediate future.

◇ **We use the present tense of the verb be + verb + ing to form the present continuous tense.**

Affirmative Statements

I <u>am</u> study<u>ing</u>.

He
She <u>is</u> work<u>ing</u>.
It

We
You <u>are</u> mak<u>ing</u> a decision
They

Negative Statements

I <u>am</u> <u>not</u> study<u>ing</u>.

He
She <u>is not</u> work<u>ing</u>.
It

We
You <u>are not</u> mak<u>ing</u> a decision.
They

We use contractions of the verb <u>be</u> in conversation.

E X A M P L E : He'<u>s</u> playing tennis right now.

Yes/No Questions

<u>Is</u> he work<u>ing</u>?

<u>Are</u> you work<u>ing</u>?

◇ **When a verb ends in <u>e</u>, drop the <u>e</u> before adding <u>ing</u>.**

E X A M P L E :	**Make**	**Making**
	Write	**Writing**

PRACTICE 7

Complete the following with the present continuous tense.

1. The butcher_____ (weigh) a steak.

PRACTICE 7

2. The detectives _____ (investigate) a murder.

3. The firemen _____ (rescue) a cat from a tree.

4. _____ you _____ (wait) for Dr. Martin?

5. The librarian _____ (reshelve) some books.

6. _____ the student _____ (do) his homework?

7. The policeman (neg.) _____ (give) the motorist a ticket.

8. The lawyer _____ (defend) his client in court.

9. The surgeon _____ (perform) an operation.

10. _____ the teachers _____ (mark) the exams?

PRACTICE 8

Andrea wants to change her job. Use the following verbs and describe what she is doing about it.

research, do, get, check, speak, read, take

1. courses
2. career counselling
3. friends
4. possible options
5. aptitude tests
6. career section of newspaper
7. employment statistics

Do you know any other useful job-hunting strategies? Discuss.

14

PRACTICE 9

Look at the following office scene and describe in complete sentences the actions of each person.

LET'S FOCUS

◇ **We use <u>be + ing</u> to describe a person's present behaviour.**

E X A M P L E : **He <u>is</u> usually serious, but he <u>is being</u> silly right now.**
She <u>is</u> usually careful, but she <u>is being</u> reckless right now.

LET'S FOCUS

We do not use a present continuous form for the following verbs.

believe	know	prefer
belong	like	* see
hate	love	understand
* have	need	want
hear		

* Certain idiomatic expressions use a present continuous form of <u>have</u> and <u>see</u>. In these expressions <u>have</u> and <u>see</u> do not have their usual meanings.

E X A M P L E :

He'<u>s</u> <u>having</u> a good time.

He'<u>s</u> <u>seeing</u> a chiropractor.

Changes In the Job Market

The job market and work situations are changing rapidly.

Demand for workers in the technological field is growing while demand for *semi-skilled* and *unskilled* workers is declining. Statistics show that more and more women are entering the job market. Workers now have greater variety in their work schedules. Many people work full-time, *part-time, flextime* or as *temps*.

More workers are *job-sharing* or *telecommuting*. Employers are seeking employees with higher levels of education. High school *dropout*s are finding it difficult to get jobs. Most jobs require a high school diploma or university degree. Today, workers need to be flexible and versatile.

DISCUSS ◆◆◆◆◆◆◆◆◆◆◆◆◆◆◆◆◆◆◆◆◆◆

Ask your partner the following questions:

1. Do you prefer to work part-time or full-time? Why?
2. Which is more important to you: a good salary or a good working environment? Why?
3. Do you prefer to work alone or with others? Why?
4. Do you prefer to work in the day or in the evening? Why?
5. Do you prefer to work indoors or outdoors? Why?

Do you and your partner have similar answers?

WORK RELATED CHARACTERISTICS

accurate	friendly	objective
aggressive	flexible	patient
ambitious	good listener	positive attitude
assertive	honest	punctual
careful	independent	reliable
confident	loyal	responsible
cooperative	motivated	tactful
creative	neat	well-groomed

WORK TOGETHER

Work with a partner and choose <u>five</u> qualities from the list in the box on the previous page that you think make someone a good:

Nurse	Waitress/waiter
Lawyer	Manager
Teacher	

Now compare your list with the lists from other groups and discuss. Give reasons for your choices.

ACTIVITY

Match the characteristic in column A with its definition in column B.

 A   B

1.	Cooperative	a.	always on time
2.	Honest	b.	correct
3.	Independent	c.	likes to work alone
4.	Well-groomed	d.	works well with others
5.	Punctual	e.	works hard to succeed
6.	Ambitious	f.	dresses neatly and well
7.	Reliable	g.	can work at something for hours
8.	Tactful	h.	always does what is expected of him/her
9.	Patient	i.	always tells the truth
10.	Accurate	j.	skillful in dealing with people

DISCUSS ◆◆◆◆◆◆◆◆◆◆◆◆◆◆◆◆◆◆◆◆◆◆◆◆◆◆◆

Studies show that people feel satisfied with their work when it suits their character.

Which of the characteristics listed on the previous page describe you at work? At leisure? Explain why there are some differences.

18

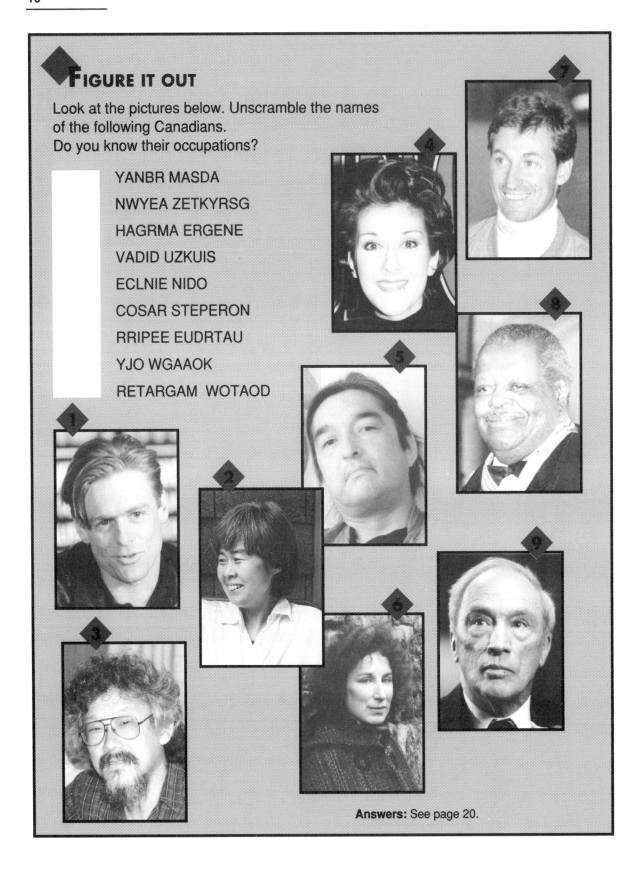

FIGURE IT OUT

Look at the pictures below. Unscramble the names of the following Canadians.
Do you know their occupations?

YANBR MASDA

NWYEA ZETKYRSG

HAGRMA ERGENE

VADID UZKUIS

ECLNIE NIDO

COSAR STEPERON

RRIPEE EUDRTAU

YJO WGAAOK

RETARGAM WOTAOD

Answers: See page 20.

GLOSSARY

admin assistant, also known as AA – a person who does office work

benefits – extras that a company provides to full-time employees (such as a health insurance plan)

browse – to look around a store without meaning to buy anything

flextime – a flexible work schedule that allows workers to start and finish at different times

hectic – extremely busy

job-sharing – an arrangement in which two people share a full-time position and its salary and benefits

part-time – work that is less than 30 hours a week

priorities – most important task or duty

qualify – to meet or have the necessary requirements

salary – fixed regular monthly or annual pay

semi-skilled – partially trained for a particular job

temps – people who work through an agency on temporary assignments for a variety of companies

telecommute – to work at home using a fax machine, computer, and telephone as links to the office

unskilled – with no formal training or certification, but able to work at a variety of jobs

IDIOMS

dropout – someone who doesn't complete a course of studies

drop out – to discontinue a course of study

in the same boat – in the same situation

in a rush – in a hurry

on the blink – out of order, not functioning properly

peak hours – busy time

tip – helpful information, advice

unwind – relax

workaholic – someone who is addicted to work

ANSWERS TO FIGURE IT OUT

Bryan Adams	—	rock singer
Wayne Gretzsky	—	hockey player
Graham Greene	—	actor
David Suzuki	—	scientist
Celine Dion	—	pop singer
Oscar Peterson	—	jazz pianist
Pierre Trudeau	—	lawyer, former Prime Minister
Joy Kogawa	—	writer
Margaret Atwood	—	writer

2 JOB HUNTING

SETTING THE SCENE

1. Where are Mr. Henderson and Mr. Galetti?

2. What are they discussing?

Mr. Henderson:	How long have you been unemployed Mr. Galetti?
Mr. Galetti:	I lost my job in January, so I've been out of work for four months now.

Mr. Henderson:	Were you *laid off?*
Mr. Galetti:	Yes. The company I worked for *relocated.*
Mr. Henderson:	What is your occupation?
Mr. Galetti:	Well, I was a *welder*, but for the last few years I was also a *foreman.*
Mr. Henderson:	What have you been doing to find work?
Mr. Galetti:	I've been reading the *want ads*, I've been *going door to door*, I've been *filling out* application forms, but there doesn't seem to be much demand for welders.
Mr. Henderson:	Have you considered *retraining*? CEC offers several retraining programmes.
Mr. Galetti:	*You can't teach an old dog new tricks.*
Mr. Henderson:	You're never too old to learn, Mr. Galetti. Try this *aptitude test* and you'll see that you have a lot of transferable skills.

Comprehension Check

1. Why is Mr. Galetti unemployed?

2. What has Mr. Galetti done to find a new job?

3. What does Mr. Henderson suggest?

LET'S FOCUS

SIMPLE PAST OF BE

We use the simple past tense to talk about past actions, facts, or habits.
These actions ended before the time of speaking.

Affirmative Statements	**Negative Statements**
I	I
He	He
She <u>was</u> on time.	She <u>was not (wasn't)</u> on time.
It	It
We	We
You <u>were</u> late.	You <u>were not (weren't)</u> late.
They	They

Yes/No Questions	**Information Questions**
<u>Was</u> she on time?	Why <u>was</u> she late?
<u>Were</u> you late?	Where <u>were</u> you?

PRACTICE 1

Complete the following with the past tense of the verb <u>be</u>.

Michelle: Where _____ you Juanita? I almost left without you.

Juanita: I'm sorry Michelle. My class _____ a little longer than usual
because my students _____ late. There _____ a delay on the
subway. And, as usual, there _____ a few students who had
questions at the end of the class.

PRACTICE 1

Michelle: One of the *drawbacks* of teaching is never really getting out of class on time. But it still beats my last job.

Juanita: What _____ your last job, Michelle?

Michelle: I _____ a general manager.

Juanita: What _____ your *duties*?

Michelle: I _____ in charge of sales and sales personnel.

Juanita: Were you responsible for hiring?

Michelle: Yes. I _____ responsible for hiring, training, and doing *performance appraisals.*

Juanita: How many people _____ you in charge of?

Michelle: I _____ in charge of 10 people.

Juanita: It sounds like it _____ an interesting job.

Michelle: Yes, it ____ very interesting and challenging. But I _____ single then and my priorities _____ different. I _____ more *career-oriented.* Now I want to spend as much time as possible with my kids. Teaching French part-time in the evenings makes that possible.

LET'S FOCUS

SIMPLE PAST TENSE OF REGULAR VERBS

We add <u>ed</u> to the simple form of regular verbs to form the simple past tense.

Affirmative Statements	**Negative Statements**
I	I
He	He
She work<u>ed</u> yesterday.	She <u>did not (didn't)</u> work yesterday.
It	It
We	We
You stud<u>ied</u> yesterday.	You <u>did not (didn't)</u> work yesterday.
They	They

Yes/No Questions	**Information Questions**
<u>Did</u> he <u>work</u>?	When <u>did</u> he <u>work</u>?
<u>Did</u> you <u>work</u>?	Where <u>did</u> he <u>work</u>?

◇ **If the verb ends in a consonant + <u>y</u> we change the <u>y</u> to <u>i</u> before we add <u>ed</u>.**

    E x a m p l e: **More than 40 people appl<u>ied</u> for the position.**

◇ **We pronounce the <u>ed</u> ending of regular verbs in the past tense in the three following different ways:**

    1.   as a separate sound <u>id</u> after verbs ending in <u>t</u> or <u>d</u>.

        E x a m p l e: The gardener plant<u>ed</u> new shrubs.

    2.   as <u>t</u> after <u>p, k, f, s, x, sh,</u> and <u>ch</u>

        E x a m p l e: The gardener pick<u>ed</u> some roses.

    3.   as <u>d</u> after a voiced sound such as <u>b, g, m, n, v,</u> and <u>w</u>.

        E x a m p l e: The gardener mow<u>ed</u> the lawn yesterday.

PRACTICE 2

Complete the following with the simple past of the verb in parentheses.

Claude: What _____ you _____ last summer? (do)

Mahesh: I _____ a job in a factory. (have)

Claude: What department _____ you _____ in? (work)

Mahesh: I _____ in shipping and receiving. (help out)

Claude: What _____ you _____ in shipping and receiving? (do)

Mahesh: I _____ and _____ boxes. (pack, label) Then I _____ the boxes into a truck. (load) Sometimes, I _____ to unload the trucks. (help)

Claude: _____ you _____ the job? (like)

Mahesh: Yeah. I _____ to the radio all day and nobody _____ me. (listen, *hassle*)

Claude: _____ you _____ a lot of money? (make)

Mahesh: I _____ enough money to pay for my tuition. (earn) The pay was a little more than *minimum wage*. My boss _____ my work and _____ me a job for this summer. (like, promise) I can get you a summer job there too, if you want.

Claude: That would be great! Thanks, Mahesh.

DISCUSS ◆◆◆◆◆◆◆◆◆◆◆◆◆◆◆◆◆◆◆◆◆◆◆

Ask your partner the following questions.

1. Did you have a summer or part-time job when you were a student?
2. What was your favourite part-time job? Why?
3. Did you ever have a job that you didn't like? Why?
4. Do you think students should have part-time jobs? Why or why not?

WORK TOGETHER

In groups of three or four suggest steps and strategies for the following job seekers.

> Recent university graduate
> High school dropout
> A woman re-entering the workforce after a 5-year absence

Who can they talk to for help? How can they gain experience?

LET'S FOCUS

SIMPLE PAST TENSE OF IRREGULAR VERBS

Many verbs do not end with <u>ed</u> in the past tense. We learn these verbs by memorizing groups with similar endings. See verb list on page 195.

Affirmative Statements	**Negative Statements**
I <u>sent</u> my resume.	I <u>did not (didn't) send</u> my resume.

Yes/No Questions	**Information Questions**
<u>Did</u> you <u>send</u> your resume?	When <u>did</u> you <u>send</u> your resume?

PRACTICE 3

Yesterday was a busy day for Carla. Look at Carla's agenda and answer the questions about what she did yesterday at work.

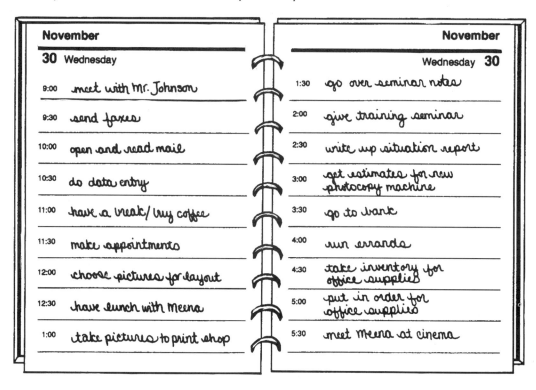

November		
30 Wednesday		Wednesday **30** November
9:00	meet with Mr. Johnson	1:30 go over seminar notes
9:30	send faxes	2:00 give training seminar
10:00	open and read mail	2:30 write up situation report
10:30	do data entry	3:00 get estimates for new photocopy machine
11:00	have a break/ buy coffee	3:30 go to bank
11:30	make appointments	4:00 run errands
12:00	choose pictures for layout	4:30 take inventory for office supplies
12:30	have lunch with Meena	5:00 put in order for office supplies
1:00	take pictures to print shop	5:30 meet Meena at cinema

1. **Did Carla meet with Meena at 9:00?**

2. **What did Carla do at 9:30?**

3. **What did she do between 10:30 and 11:30?**

4. **When did Carla have lunch? Did she eat alone?**

5. **Did Carla attend a training seminar?**

6. **Where did Carla go in the afternoon?**

7. **What did Carla do at 5:00?**

8. **Did Carla buy a new photocopy machine?**

9. **What did Carla do at break time?**

10. **What did Carla do at 4:30?**

PRACTICE 4

Complete the following sentences about the accomplishments
of these well-known Canadians.
Use the simple past tense of the verb.

1. Lucy Maude Montgomery (1874-1942) _____(be) a successful
author from Prince Edward Island. She _____ (write) over
20 novels, but her most famous is *Anne of Green Gables*.
This novel tells the story of a high-spirited young girl in P.E.I.

2. Physician Henry Norman Bethune (1890-1939), _____ (come)
from Gravenhurst, Ontario. He _____(is) a surgeon. Bethune
_____ (give up) his medical practice in 1935. During the Spanish
Civil War he_____(go) to Spain and _____(set up) a blood transfusion
unit. He _____(spend) the last years of his life working in China.
Bethune is considered a hero in China today.

3. Emily Carr (1871-1945) _____(come) from Victoria B.C.
She _____(get) her training as a painter in San Francisco.
In 1893 she _____(set up) a studio in Victoria. During the
late 1920s Carr's paintings _____ (become) very similar in
style to that of the Group of Seven.

4. Timothy Eaton (1834-1907) _____(be) the founder of the
T. Eaton Co. department stores. He _____(immigrate) to
Canada from Ireland in 1854. Timothy Eaton _____ (change)
the dry-goods business. He _____(sell) goods at a fixed
price and _____(introduce) catalogue sales in 1884.

5. On Oct. 5, 1985, Marc Garneau, a scientist and astronaut from
Quebec City, _____(become) the first Canadian in space.
He _____(fly) aboard the U.S. Space Shuttle *Challenger*.

LET'S FOCUS

PRESENT PERFECT TENSE

We use the present perfect tense to indicate that an action began in the past and is still continuing in the present; or to describe actions that were completed in the past at an unspecified time or date.

| I
You
We
They | have + past participle | <u>I've worked</u> here for six months. |
| He
She | has + past participle | <u>Has</u> he ever <u>owned</u> a small business?
Yes, <u>he's</u> <u>owned</u> a franchise. |

1. The word <u>ever</u> also helps us to talk about actions that occurred at an indefinite time in the past. It is only used in questions and negative sentences.
2. The word <u>never</u> is commonly used for negative answers.

   E X A M P L E :   Have you ever taken a computer course?
   No, I haven't ever taken a computer course.
   or
   No, I have never taken a computer course.

PRACTICE 5

Work with a partner. Construct sentences using the following information and the present perfect tense.

E X A M P L E :   **Giovanni never (work) in Canada.**
Giovanni has never worked in Canada.

   1. He (read) the want ads.

   2. He (visit) several employers.

PRACTICE 5

3. He (take) a few courses to upgrade his qualifications.

4. He (begin) to feel more confident.

5. Giovanni's friend (promise) *to keep an eye open* for a good job.

PRACTICE 6

Complete the following with the appropriate form of the verb in parentheses.
Choose from simple present, simple past, or present perfect.
More than one form may be correct.

Mahesh _____(work) for the same company during the summer holidays

for the last 2 years. He _____(do) a good job and his boss, Mr. Chang,

_____(be) happy with his work. Each summer Mr. Chang _____(give)

Mahesh a raise and _____ (promise) to rehire him this summer. In fact,

Mr. Chang _____(ask) Mahesh to work part-time after school. But

Mahesh's parents _____(tell) him that they don't want him to work

during the school year. Although he always _____ (do) well in school

they are afraid his grades might suffer if he works part-time. Even

though Mahesh _____(assure) them that he won't let his grades drop,

they _____(refuse) to let him work part-time.

WORK TOGETHER

Find out about your partner's accomplishments. Form a question in the present perfect tense.

Have you ever...

- counsel anyone
- assemble anything
- give information
- ship something somewhere
- take telephone orders
- handle large sums of money
- care for children, the handicapped, or the elderly
- teach or give instruction
- paint anything

- write a report
- supervise workers
- manage a project
- analyze data
- give a presentation
- create a new way of doing something
- do research
- build and repair things
- organize a major event

LET'S FOCUS

PRESENT PERFECT CONTINUOUS

We use the present perfect continuous when the action began at some unspecified time in the past and is still continuing in the present.

Affirmative Statements	**Negative Statements**
I You <u>have been working</u> all day. We They	I You <u>haven't been working</u> all day. We They
He She <u>has been working</u> all day.	He She <u>hasn't been</u> working all day.

LET'S FOCUS

What <u>have</u> you <u>been</u> <u>doing</u> since last year?

I
You
We <u>have been working</u> steadily since last year.
They

◇ **In spoken English, the present perfect and present perfect continuous are often expressed in a contracted form.**

E X A M P L E :   **What've you been up to?**

I've been looking for work.

She's been helping me with my resume.

PRACTICE 7

What have the following people been doing?

E X A M P L E :   student: **He's been reading all afternoon.**

1. pilot
2. receptionist
3. waitress
4. pharmacist
5. traffic cop
6. cashier
7. teacher
8. hair stylist
9. cook
10. doctor

LET'S FOCUS

SINCE AND FOR

Some words which we use with the present
perfect tense are:

<u>Since</u> + a date/time to indicate when an action
began.

**E X A M P L E : He has worked here <u>since</u> the
company first opened.**

<u>For</u> + a number or a quantity adverb to indicate
the duration of an activity.

E X A M P L E : He has worked here <u>for</u> many years.

PRACTICE 8

Complete these sentences with either <u>since</u> or <u>for</u>.

1. She's worked here_____six years.

2. They've been discussing the new contract_____a month.

3. I've been waiting for an interview___more than a month.

4. Have you worked at this company ____1992?

5. He's been designing a new product___last year.

6. She's had a new job___a week.

7. We've been calling the office _____yesterday.

8. I've been studying that software programme_____the last few
months.

LET'S FOCUS

JUST, ALREADY, BEFORE

The present perfect is often used to talk about an action that has been completed recently. The action may have been completed a few minutes ago or many weeks before the time of speaking. It depends on the speaker's point of view. No time phrases are used with these words.

I've just finished my project. Now I can take a break.

I've just graduated. Now I'm going to look for a job.

I don't need to read that book because I've read it before.

She's already had her appointment with the career counsellor.

◇ **We put already immediately after the auxiliary verb have or at the end of the sentence.**

PRACTICE 9

Choose between the present perfect and the present perfect continuous.
In some cases both answers may be correct.

E X A M P L E : **The class has already begun.**

1. He_____(try) to fix the machine for two hours and he's still having difficulty.

2. I____(use) this kind of computer software many times.

3. _____ you ever _____ (operate) this kind of machine?

4. We_____(not look) for work for very long.

PRACTICE 9

5. I _____(send out) my resume several times since last March.

6. He_____(read) the classified ads every day.

7. She_____(just/start) to look for work.

8. _____you _____(already/have) many job interviews?

9. I_____(study) this manual all day.

10. I don't have any Canadian work experience because I_____(just/ arrive).

LET'S FOCUS

YET

We use yet:

1. to indicate that something has not been achieved or completed.

   E X A M P L E : **Mr. Galetti hasn't got a new job yet?**

2. when we want to explain that it is too early to expect completion.

   E X A M P L E : **Mr. Galetti hasn't started the retraining yet. It begins next week.**

3. when we feel something is taking too long to complete.

   E X A M P L E : **Hasn't Juanita come out of class yet? The class was over 10 minutes ago.**

◇ **We put yet at the end of a negative sentence or a question.**

PRACTICE 10

Complete the following sentences using <u>ever</u>, <u>never</u>, <u>just</u>, <u>already</u>, <u>before</u>, and <u>yet</u>.

E X A M P L E : Have you <u>ever</u> worked on this type of computer before?

1. Where have you worked____?
2. I've worked in a laboratory, but I've _____used this kind of machine _____.
3. He hasn't filled out the application form_____.
4. I haven't spoken to a UI counsellor ____.
5. Have you _____completed the course?
6. Yes, I've____completed the course.
7. Have you ____worked as part of a team?
8. I've _____worked as a project supervisor.
9. I've_____applied for work at this company twice. Should I apply again?
10. I'm so happy! I've_____found a job!

PRACTICE 11

Use the present perfect or the simple past. The time phrases in the sentences will help you to choose the best tense.

1. I____(get) the job last week.
2. He____(work) in that factory since 1989.

PRACTICE 11

3. The committee_____ (promote) her last year.

4. I_____(commute) to the office since last August.

5. She _____(update) her resume several times during the last ten years.

6. _____you_____already (finish)?

7. I _____(complete) the survey an hour ago.

8. What kind of work experience_____you_____(have)?

9. He_____(enroll) in three computer courses last year.

10. _____you_____(teach) mathematics before?

ROLE PLAY

Take turns as the job applicant. Use the present perfect and present perfect continuous to ask and answer questions relevant to the positions.

Begin the questions with: "Have you ever..."

E X A M P L E :   *"Have you ever worked with children?"*

Position:

High School Math Teacher	Store Clerk	Nanny
Waitress	Truck Driver	Carpenter

◆ WORK TOGETHER

In groups of three or four read the following and decide together who gets the job.

Ms. Fernandez is the manager of a major department store. She needs to hire a new sales manager. The sales manager must have the following qualifications:

1. degree/certificate in business administration
2. sales experience
3. good communication skills

Read the brief biographies of the 4 applicants for the position described below.

CANDIDATE #1: Peter Stevens
EDUCATION: M.B.A.
EXPERIENCE: 2 years general manager of fast food restaurant
SKILLS: computer literate
APPEARANCE: very neat and well-groomed
PERSONALITY: cold
MANNER: businesslike, abrupt

CANDIDATE #2: Lia Stavros
EDUCATION: B.A. (major in marketing)
EXPERIENCE: sales clerk for 4 years in small boutique
APPEARANCE: casual
PERSONALITY: easy-going
MANNER: friendly, a bit restless

CANDIDATE #3: Debbie Kwan
EDUCATION: Diploma in Computer and Business Applications
EXPERIENCE: 2 years as head bank teller
SKILLS: accounting experience
APPEARANCE: well-groomed
PERSONALITY: self-assured
MANNER: maintained eye contact

CANDIDATE #4: Feroz Khan
EDUCATION: Bachelor of Commerce
EXPERIENCE: 5 years managing family business
SKILLS: able to use various computer systems
APPEARANCE: neat and well-groomed
PERSONALITY: friendly
MANNER: self-assured

JOB HUNTING

When we are job hunting we need to use many different strategies if we hope to achieve success. Two tools that are vital when we have found a position we think may be suitable are the covering letter and the resume. These serve to introduce you to a prospective employer. It is, therefore, essential that they create a good impression. The following are a number of tips for writing good covering letters and resumes.

Covering Letter Checklist

1. Include your address and phone number.

2. Choose the appropriate salutation.

3. Use a business-like format.

4. Highlight key strengths and abilities.

5. State your relevant education and experience.

6. Keep it brief, two or three paragraphs.

7. Mention the ad or person who referred you (if applicable).

Tips for Writing a Winning Resume

1. Emphasize the skills you possess that would be an asset for the job you are seeking.

2. Be truthful and write in a brief and concise manner.

3. Outline your work experience, education, references, skills, etc.

4. Use action words.

5. Write in a businesslike manner.

6. Give dates.

7. Proofread for typing, grammatical and spelling errors.

DISCUSS ◆◆◆◆◆◆◆◆◆◆◆◆◆◆◆◆◆◆◆◆◆◆

1. Why do we write resumes and covering letters?

2. What should a covering letter include?

3. Have you ever written a resume or a covering letter?

4. What do covering letters and resumes include in your country of origin?

DISCUSS ◆◆◆◆◆◆◆◆◆◆◆◆◆◆◆◆◆◆◆◆◆◆◆

Here are samples of two covering letters. How would you improve them?

After discussing the letters with a partner, combine the best qualities of both samples and write your own covering letter.

---

123 Oak Avenue
Toronto, Ontario
M6G 2B3
April 7, 1994

To Whom It May Concern;

I am applying for the position of Multicultural Workplace Instructor at the Queen Elizabeth Hospital. As you will see from my resume, I am currently teaching several courses for The Toronto Board of Education, Continuing Education and I am a member of C.U.P.E. Local 1234.

Over the past several years, I have demonstrated my ability to design materials and curricula which effectively meet the needs of learners at a wide variety of levels and situations. In addition, I have taught several classes in the workplace and recognize the importance of being able to work with learners at different levels and with different personal and work related needs.

I believe I have both the qualifications and experience necessary to fill the position of Multicultural Workplace Instructor at Queen Elizabeth Hospital. I can be reached at (416) 123-4567 during the afternoon and evening. I look forward to hearing from you.

Sincerely yours,

Emilia Rojas

---

73 Clarence Street
Edmonton, Alberta
E4P 2N7

May 6, 1994

ABC Electric Company
123 Jones Avenue
Edmonton, Alberta
E7K 2F3

Attention: Ms Jana Korchek

I am applying for the position in the Edmonton Gazette. I feel I would be excellent for this position since I have had a great deal of experience in this area.

As you can see from my resumé, I have just completed an upgrading course in computers and I feel this would be useful too.

I look forward to hearing from you. I can be reached at 432-5678.

Afuah Dynulwa

DISCUSS ◆◆◆◆◆◆◆◆◆◆◆◆◆◆◆◆◆◆◆◆◆

Here are two resumes. The resume on this page is set up in *chronological* format and the resume on the following page is set up in *functional* format. Discuss the advantages and disadvantages of each type. How would you improve them? After your discussion, write or revise your own resume.

Resume

Name: Marushka Zandorra
Address: 123 Albert Avenue, Calgary, Alberta A7G 2B5
Telephone: (403) 123-4567

Employment

1990-Present   Alberta Board of Education   ESL Instructor
               Have taught a wide variety of classes including Basic Bilingual, Beginner II, Intermediate, Advanced and TEOFL.

1988-1990   Senior Polytechnic Institute, Krakow   Director of Studies
               Hired and trained ESL instructors, developed curriculum, taught a wide variety of levels and evaluated learners' levels.

1984-1988   Krakow Institute of Languages   Registrar
               Managed office, hired ESL instructors, developed curriculum and evaluated learners' language levels.

1981-1984   Krakow Language School   ESL Instructor

Education

1992   Job Search Skills Instructor's Certificate
        Toronto Board of Education

1991   Practical Approaches to Facilitating Literacy
        Toronto Board of Education

1988   RSA Certificate
        Bell College, England

1984   Masters of Education, Multicultural Education
        Krakow Institute for Studies in Education

1979   Teacher's Degree: ESL Specialist
        Krakow Teachers Institute

— References supplied upon request —

Leung Ting Mei

123 Maple Road   Telephone: (604) 567-8910
Vancouver, British Columbia
B8N 5F7

Skills:

C.A.E. specialist. Solid Modeling Design and Drafting.

Able to work on a project from conceptual design to final drawings as well as support the fabrication stage.

Able to work to schedule and meet deadlines consistently.

Good knowledge of D.O. practices, A.N.S.I. and Military STD.

Able to work well as part of a team and to motivate others.

Experience:

Y & X Engineering   1985-1990

HONG KONG

Designer/draftsman

Responsible for job estimating, scheduling and planning, proposal estimates, assigning work, checking, co-ordinating projects with other departments.

Education:

Seneca College. Drafting Refreshment course.	1994
Hong Kong Institute of Science	1982-1985
Royal Military College	1979-1982

Volunteer Positions:

West Mountain Children's Center   1992-1994

Mathematics tutor

Soccer coach

References supplied on demand

WORK TOGETHER

Work with a partner and write up a list of tips for a successful interview. Include information about the following:

punctuality, appearance, interview questions and answers.

WORK TOGETHER

The workplace has changed a lot over the last 30 years.
In groups of three or four discuss some of these changes. Use the present perfect whenever possible.

EXAMPLE: **In many offices the computer has replaced the typewriter.**

ACTIVITY

Look at the following scene of a busy restaurant. What has each person in the scene just done?

ACTIVITY

Look at the following ads and write the full form of the abbreviations.

1. $32K _____
2. immed _____
3. ass't _____
4. req'd _____
5. PT/FT _____
6. exper _____
7. exec _____
8. flex hrs _____
9. incl _____

GENERAL MANAGER

The Bain Co-Op general manager plans, directs and controls the overall management of the co-op. Strong organizational and administrative skills. Experience in property management. Good supervisory skills and experience in personnel management. Familiarity with computerized word processing, spread sheets, data management and accounting software a definite asset. Good interpersonal skills. Requires 5 years experience in comparable organizations. 40 hours/week, some evening work. $45-50K + good benefits. Deadline June 20. Start date August 1/94. Apply in writing to Bain Co-Operative Apts. Inc., 100 Bain Ave., #29L, Toronto, M4K 1E8, or fax 416-463-0829.

SECRETARY, Exec Ass't strong dicta, excel WP 5.1, typing 70 WPM+, some bookkeeping asset. Major firm in Weston, Approx $32K. Star Box 7747

LEGAL SECRETARY req'd for partner in Mississauga law firm. This is a permanent part time position (3 days/wk) which may be increased to full time in the future. Applicants must have min of 5 yrs of recent corporate-commercial exper & a thorough working knowledge of WordPerfect 5.1. Please FAX resumes to the attention of Human Resources Department, 905-276-4802

R.N., Lab Tech, PT/FT in different areas, 2nd language an asset. Send résumé: 80 Travail Rd. Unit 1, Markham, L3S 3H9.

R.N./Physical Therapist/Occupational Therapist. Temp/perm positions in USA. All expenses paid. Internet. 416-480-2461

FLORAL designer exper Scarb. E., flex hrs, FT/PT. Immed. 416-265-6867

CONTROLLER with 4 yrs exper Computer knowledge essential. Position incl computer & manual bookkeeping. Call w/salary expectations: 416-350-5555 9097#.

GLOSSARY

aptitude test – a test to find out what natural skills you have

chronological – in order of occurrence

duties – responsibilities

fill out – to complete

foreman – supervisor in a factory

functional – emphasizing skills

go door to door – to go from one house or place of business to another

laid off – let go from a job because of lack of work and overstaffing

minimum wage – the lowest wage that can be legally paid

networking – making contacts through friends and relatives

performance appraisal – progress report on an employee's strengths and weaknesses in his/her job

relocate – to move operations to another location. A person moves for employment reasons

retraining – preparing someone for a job in another field

to be career-oriented – to consider career decisions and plans most important

want ads – advertisements offering employment

welder – operates welding equipment to fuse metal parts together

IDIOMS

drawbacks – disadvantages

hassle – to annoy

to keep an eye open – watch carefully for

You can't teach an old dog new tricks – it is difficult to teach people new skills as they grow older

UNIT 3

KEEPING HEALTHY

SETTING THE SCENE

1. Why is Ting Mei at the Newcomer Services office?

2. What is he asking the receptionist for?

Receptionist:	Newcomer Services, how can I help you?
Ting Mei:	I would like to get a health card.

Receptionist: You can apply for a health card at the Ministry of Health Office. Take your birth certificate, Canada Immigration visa and passport with you.

Ting Mei: Does my health card also cover my children?

Receptionist: All members of your family must have their own coverage. Take their documents with you. The government officer will give you information about registering them. You'll get a temporary card immediately and you'll receive a permanent plastic card in the mail.

LATER . . .

Officer: Here is a temporary health card. You should receive your permanent plastic card in a few weeks.

Ting Mei: Can I use the card throughout Canada?

Officer: If you are visiting another province you can use the card in an emergency. However, if you move to another province you should apply for a new card as soon as possible.

Ting Mei: What medical services does it cover?

Officer: It covers basic hospital charges, doctors' fees and some treatments prescribed by a doctor.

Ting Mei: Does it cover dental work or drugs?

Officer: No. Health care does not cover treatments or services provided by people who do not have a licence to practise medicine. This *pamphlet* should answer any other questions you may have.

Comprehension Check

1. What does the receptionist tell Ting Mei to do?

2. What does he need to take to the Ministry of Health?

3. What can he use his health card for?

LET'S FOCUS

MODAL AUXILIARIES

<u>Can</u>, <u>must</u>, <u>should</u>, <u>may</u>, <u>might</u>, <u>could</u>, and <u>would</u> are modal auxiliaries. These modal auxiliaries have many uses. The following chart shows some of the ways we use these modals in talking about present and future situations. Remember we use modals with a second verb. The second verb is in the simple form. We do not change the form of the modal auxiliaries for the different persons.

Modal	Use	Example
can	present ability or opportunity	You <u>can use</u> your health card at the doctor's office. You <u>cannot</u> <u>(can't)</u> <u>use</u> your health card for dental services.

50

LET'S FOCUS

Modal	Use	Example
can	request	<u>Can</u> you <u>help</u> me?
could	polite request	<u>Could</u> you <u>help</u> me?
would	polite request	<u>Would</u> you <u>call</u> the nurse?
	polite offer	<u>Would</u> you <u>like</u> a cup of coffee?
may	possibility	The medication <u>may have</u> some side effects.
	permission	<u>May</u> I <u>see</u> your health card?
might	possibility	You <u>might feel</u> drowsy.
must	necessity	You <u>must have</u> your own health card.
		<u>Must</u> I <u>take</u> my health card each time I go to the doctor?
have to	necessity	You <u>have to make</u> an appointment to see the doctor.
		We <u>don't have to</u> make an appointment to go to a walk-in clinic.
		Do I <u>have to get</u> private insurance to cover dental costs?
should	advice	You <u>shouldn't take</u> any medication prescribed for someone else.
		<u>Should</u> I <u>take</u> these pills before meals?
ought to	advice	I <u>ought to quit</u> smoking.

PRACTICE 1

Complete the following with the appropriate modal: <u>must</u>, <u>should</u>, <u>can</u>, or <u>may</u>.

MEDICAL SERVICES IN CANADA

You _____ only go to the emergency department of the nearest hospital if you are seriously injured or ill. In many Canadian cities you _____ dial 9-1-1 to get ambulances and other emergency services immediately. In other communities you _____ dial "0" and ask the operator to send an ambulance. If it is not a true emergency you _____ pay a service fee for the ambulance. In some provinces you _____ pay for part of the service even if it is a true emergency.

Patients _____ go to a walk-in *clinic* for minor injuries or ailments. Doctors and nurses at walk-in clinics see patients on a *first-come, first-served* basis rather than an appointment basis.

Everyone _____ have a "family" doctor. This doctor _____ treat ordinary medical problems. The family doctor _____ keep a medical record for each patient. Patients _____ go to the family doctor for a physical or *checkup* at least once a year. If a patient needs special treatment the family doctor _____ recommend another doctor. In most cases you _____ make an appointment to see the doctor. People often ask relatives, friends, or co-workers to recommend a good doctor. Women _____ feel more comfortable with a woman doctor. Patients _____ change doctors at any time. They _____ also seek another opinion from a different doctor. Patients often do this if they _____ have an operation or if they have a serious illness.

PRACTICE 2

Complete the following dialogue:

Use <u>can</u>, <u>may</u>, <u>would</u>, or <u>could</u> to make polite requests.

Receptionist: _____ I help you?

Meena: I've had a very sore throat for several days. _____ I see a doctor today?

Receptionist: Certainly. The doctor can see you in about twenty minutes. _____ you mind waiting?

Meena: Not at all. I thought it might be longer.

Receptionist: _____ you please fill out this form? _____ I see your health card?

Meena: Oh no! I forgot my health card. _____ I bring it tomorrow?

Receptionist: I'm sorry. I must see your health card because this is your first visit. _____ you go home and get it?

Meena: Sure. I'll be right back.

LATER . . .

Receptionist: _____ you like a cup of tea while you're waiting?

Meena: Thanks it might make my throat feel better.

Dr. Chen: _____ you please step into my office? I'll see you now. _____ you shut the door? Thanks.

PRACTICE 3

Sue Yen and Ting Mei, her husband, are expecting their first child in a few months. Today they are visiting the hospital to get some information about what to expect and what to do when the baby arrives.

Here are some of the *midwife's* answers to their questions. What do you think the questions were?

EXAMPLE: Sue Yen: When should I come to the hospital?

Midwife: Come to the hospital when the pains are about 20 minutes apart.

Ting Mei: _____?

Midwife: Bring a suitcase with some clothes, slippers, a toothbrush and, of course, clothes for the baby.

Sue Yen: _____?

Midwife: When you take the baby home, wrap it warmly and put on a knitted bonnet.

Ting Mei: _____?

Midwife: No, you don't have to be in the delivery room but it's a great experience.

Sue Yen: _____?

Midwife: Yes. If you feel fine, there's no reason why you can't work until the baby's born.

Ting Mei: _____?

Midwife: Well, Sue Yen can take 24 weeks of leave with unemployment insurance or you can take 10 weeks and she can take 14 weeks.

PRACTICE 3

Ting Mei: _____?

Midwife: Yes, you can take the leave at the same time or Sue Yen can take it first and you can take it later.

Sue Yen: _____?

Midwife: You should be able to take the baby home after 24 hours.

PRACTICE 4

Look at the following situations. With your partner use <u>can</u>, <u>should</u>, or <u>must</u> to give advice, make recommendations, and show necessity. You may use negatives.

E X A M P L E : **Juanita has a headache.**
She should take an aspirin. (<u>or</u>) She should lie down.

1. Belita has a bad cold.
2. Meena broke her leg.
3. Carla lost her health card.
4. Simon is allergic to penicillin.
5. Andrea is afraid to go to the dentist.
6. Juanita and Pedro have food poisoning.
7. Pedro has a sharp pain in his side.
8. Simon doesn't think his doctor is competent.
9. Belita likes ice cream but it makes her sick.
10. On her way home from work Carla saw a _hit-and-run_ accident.

WORK TOGETHER

Look at the following signs in a doctor's office. With your partner ask and answer questions about the signs. Use modals in your questions and your answers.

> **EXAMPLE:**
>
> **A:** What do I have to do before I enter the office?
>
> **B:** You must remove your boots before entering the office.

PLEASE REMOVE YOUR BOOTS BEFORE ENTERING OFFICE.

NO SMOKING

NEW PATIENTS MUST SHOW HEALTH CARDS.

ALL PATIENTS MUST REGISTER AT FRONT DESK UPON ARRIVAL.

Please help yourself to tea or coffee.

Please advise the office if you are going to miss an appointment

LET'S GET SET

1. Why is Bobby visiting Dr. Deol?

Dr. Deol: Hello, Bobby, how are you feeling today?

Bobby: My throat is still a bit sore, but I can swallow now.

Dr. Deol: Well, just open wide and I'll look at your throat.
The infection is clearing up nicely. Is he still coughing?

Mrs. Sharma: He isn't coughing as much.

Dr. Deol: Good. Make sure he takes all the medication.
The infection ought to disappear completely in a little while.

Mrs. Sharma: Thank you doctor. Should I make another appointment for next week?

Dr. Deol: No, that won't be necessary.
Bobby should be fine and back at school next week.

Mrs. Sharma: Thank you so much doctor. I'm glad I brought Bobby to see you. The other doctor dismissed my concerns about Bobby's sore throat.

Dr. Deol: Remember Mrs. Sharma: if you are not satisfied with a doctor's *diagnosis* or treatment, you should get a second opinion.

Comprehension Check

1. What is wrong with Bobby?

2. What instructions does the doctor give Mrs. Sharma?

3. What branch of medicine do you think Dr. Deol specializes in?

 LET'S FOCUS

MODAL AUXILIARIES

Modal	Use	Example
should	prediction	You <u>should</u> get your health card in two weeks
		You <u>shouldn't</u> have any problems.
		Belita left an hour ago. She <u>should</u> be arriving soon <u>shouldn't</u> she?
ought to	prediction	You <u>ought to</u> feel better soon if you take two of these tablets.
must	assumption	John comes from Portugal. He <u>must</u> speak Portuguese.
	We use <u>must</u> to express an assumption based on facts we have. The assumption may not be true.	I've waited an hour. David <u>mustn't</u> be coming.

 The question form is seldom used with <u>ought to</u> because it is very long.

PRACTICE 5

Use <u>must</u>, <u>should</u>, or <u>ought</u> <u>to</u> to complete the following assumptions and predictions.

E x a m p l e :   **You studied at McGill Medical School. You <u>must</u> know my sister, Dr. Maria Ramirez. She studied there too.**

1. Take this medicine for one week. You_____feel better by then. If not, then make another appointment to see me.

2. We've been waiting in emergency for 3 hours. We _____ be able to see a doctor soon.

3. The Hospital for Sick Children is world famous. It _____ be an excellent Hospital.

4. Mrs. Sharma, please give your child 2 tablets. His temperature _____ go down within half an hour.

5. That's a very badly sprained ankle. Keep it elevated and take these pain killers and it _____ not hurt so much.

6. Meena, that nurse _____know you. She keeps looking at you and smiling.

7. I called 911. The ambulance_____be here soon. Keep calm.

8. You_____ be tired, Dr. Chow. You've been working all night.

9. Bobby's forehead is very hot. He _____ have a fever.

DISCUSS ◆◆◆◆◆◆◆◆◆◆◆◆◆

There are many "home remedies" for common ailments such as the common cold. Some people recommend "chicken soup" or a drink of "hot water with a little honey and lemon". Do you know of any "home remedies" for these common ailments?

1. hiccups
2. insomnia
3. a headache
4. a sore throat
5. warts

6. pimples
7. wrinkles
8. arthritis
9. a hangover
10. aching feet

The Hospital for Sick Children

In 1875, a group of women in Toronto started the Hospital for Sick Children. The organizer of the project was Elizabeth McMaster. Today the hospital, which is also known as "Sick Kids" is one of the best *pediatric* hospitals in the world. The hospital treats 280,000 patients annually. Children come from all over the world for treatment at Sick Kids.

The Hospital for Sick Children has one of the largest pediatric research institutes in the world. The research institute conducts research on a wide range of illnesses and disorders.

Researchers at the hospital have discovered many treatment techniques. They have made some significant *advances* in the *diagnosis* and treatment of many *chronic illnesses*. *Surgeons* at "Sick Kids" have *pioneered* many surgical procedures. One of the procedures they have perfected is the "blue baby operation" which has saved the lives of numerous children. This operation involves changing the position of the great *vessels* of the heart.

Comprehension Check

Indicate whether the following statements are <u>true</u> or <u>false</u>.

1. The Hospital for Sick Children only treats Canadian children.

2. A group of men founded the hospital in 1860.

3. The Hospital for Sick Children has one of the largest pediatric research institutes in the world.

4. Researchers at the hospital have made important advances.

5. Surgeons at "Sick Kids" were the first to use many new procedures.

DISCUSS ◆◆◆◆◆◆◆◆◆◆◆◆◆◆◆◆◆◆◆

In small groups make a list of some of the most recent advances in medicine. Pick two of the more controversial advances from your list and debate the advantages and disadvantages. Be sure to use modal auxiliaries to make your argument more persuasive.

ACTIVITY

Match the health care specialist in column A with the area of specialization in column B.

 A   B

1. A Surgeon | **a.** family doctor

2. A Pediatrician | **b.** specializes in treating heart problems

3. An Opthalmologist | **c.** specializes in treating women's health concerns

4. An Obstetrician **d.** specializes in treating mental disorders

5. A Cardiologist **e.** performs operations

6. A Psychiatrist **f.** specializes in treating children's illnesses

7. A Chiropractor **g.** specializes in treating skin problems

8. A Dermatologist **h.** specializes in treating back problems

9. A General Practitioner **i.** specializes in treating pregnant women

10. A Gynecologist **j.** specializes in treating eye problems

ACTIVITY

Which of the following items should go into a First Aid Kit?

GLOSSARY

advances – progress
checkup – complete medical examination
clinic – place for medical examination, advice or treatment
chronic illness – illness that continues over a long period of time
diagnosis – statement of recognition for identification of a disease
midwife – trained person who assists at childbirth
pediatric – for children
pamphlet – a small information booklet
pioneer – to be the first to do something
surgeons – doctors who operate
vessel – passageway for blood

IDIOMS

first come, first served – to receive service in order of arrival
hit-and-run – person causing an accident leaves the scene of the accident immediately

4 SAFETY FIRST

SETTING THE SCENE

1. What is Meena doing?

2. What is Simon helping her to prepare for?

Meena: I don't think I'll pass the test tomorrow.

Simon: Don't be silly, you'll do just fine. Turn right at the next street.

Meena: I think I'm getting better at the turns now.

Simon: That was a good turn, but there was a stop sign at that intersection. You should have come to a complete stop before you turned.

Meena: We're coming up to a yield sign. Do I have to stop?

Simon: No. Slow down and be prepared to stop if there's any traffic.

Meena: You're a very patient driving instructor.

Simon: Well I've had lots of practice. I had to teach all my brothers and sisters.

Meena: Could we practise parallel parking? I can't *get the hang of it.*

Simon: Sure. Just pull a little ahead of that car and then back in behind it. Remember to check over your shoulder and use the mirrors.

Meena: Whew! I did it.

Simon: Congratulations. That was perfect. Now let's go over to the mall to practise backing in and out of parking spaces.

Comprehension Check

1. What mistake did Meena make at the stop sign?

2. What does Meena want to practise?

3. What should you do when you are parallel parking?

LET'S FOCUS

PAST TENSE MODALS

Modals have many different uses. For example, the modal <u>could</u>, also discussed in Unit 3, has a present meaning and a past meaning. The modals listed below have special past tense forms.

<u>Could</u> may be used as the past tense of <u>can</u>.

> **EXAMPLE:** **I <u>can</u> drive a car.**
> **I <u>could</u> drive a car last year.**

<u>Must</u> has no past tense.

<u>Have to</u> has the same meaning as <u>must</u> when <u>must</u> is used to express obligation.

> **EXAMPLE:** **I <u>must</u> pay this bill before tomorrow.**
> **I <u>have to</u> pay this bill before tomorrow.**

We use the past tense of <u>have to</u> to express the past of <u>must</u>.

> **EXAMPLE:** **I <u>must</u> speak to Meena before she leaves.**
> **I <u>had to</u> speak to Meena before she left.**
> **I <u>didn't have to</u> go to the hospital.**

In order to express the past tense of <u>should</u>, we use
<u>should + have + past participle</u>

> **EXAMPLE:** **I <u>should</u> see a doctor.**
> **I <u>should have seen</u> a doctor.**

PRACTICE 1

Put the modals in parentheses into the past form.

Peter: Where have you two been? I've been waiting here for half an hour. You _____ (should/call).

PRACTICE 1

Belita: We went to our Tae Kwon Do class.
The pay phone was out of order so we _____ (can/call) you.

Peter: Tae Kwon Do? I didn't know you were taking self-defense. How long have you been taking classes?

Sally: We've only had a couple of lessons. We _____ (should/do) this a long time ago.

Peter: If I ever need protection I'll know who to call.

Belita: Well, I wouldn't go that far. All that exercise was tiring.
I_____(have to/stop) a few times during the practice.

Sally: So did I. I_____(can/keep up with) the instructor. We'll ache all over tomorrow. We _____ (should/go) at a slower pace.

Peter: I think it's great that you're taking martial arts. It helps to build inner and outer strength. It's also a good way to stay in shape.

PRACTICE 2

With your partner complete the following sentences with a modal and a verb. Use <u>could</u>, <u>should have</u>, or <u>had to</u>. Use negatives if necessary. Remember to use the simple form for the second verb.

E X A M P L E :   **Laura was afraid to walk home at night.**

She <u>should have taken</u> Tae Kwon Do lessons.

1. Jane owed $1000 in medical bills.
   She _____.

PRACTICE 2

2. Wan Ming lost his wallet with all his identification and his health card.

He _____ .

3. Paul didn't read his prescription carefully. He got very sick.

He _____ .

4. Istavan lost a library book.

He _____ .

5. Mr. Galetti hurt his back at work.

He _____ .

DISCUSS ◆◆◆◆◆◆◆◆◆◆◆◆◆◆◆◆◆◆◆◆

1. Did you ever have to do something you didn't want to do because it was for your own good?

E X A M P L E : **I had to take <u>Cod Liver Oil</u>.**

2. Is there anything that you could do when you were younger that you can't do now?

3. Have you ever had an accident? What could you have done to avoid it?

LET'S GET SET

1. Where are Andrea and Mr. Galetti?

2. What are they doing?

Andrea:	Well, how did the interview go?
Mr. Galetti:	It went really well. I got the job.
Andrea:	That's great Dad! Tell me all about it.
Mr. Galetti:	Mr. Taylor the boss said that I could start tomorrow. I'll be working in the warehouse. Mr. Taylor warned me that there's a lot of heavy work loading and unloading trucks. But I told him that I wasn't afraid of hard work.
Andrea:	All that physical activity will be good exercise.
Mr. Galetti:	It sure will. Mr. Taylor showed me around and explained not only the job but all the safety regulations.
Andrea:	Safety regulations?
Mr. Galetti:	Yes. He said that I had to wear safety boots, and that I couldn't smoke in the shipping area. He also said that I should bend my knees when I'm lifting heavy boxes.

Comprehension Check

1. When will Mr. Galetti start working?

2. What kind of job did Mr. Galetti get?

3. Where will he work?

4. What are some of the safety regulations?

LET'S FOCUS

DIRECT AND INDIRECT SPEECH

In writing when we want to indicate that someone is speaking we use quotation marks (" ") around the speaker's words. However, when we want to express the meaning of a person's words without using exact speech we use indirect speech. To indicate indirect speech we change the subject of the subordinate clause. We also change the tense of the verb in the subordinate clause.

Direct Speech		Indirect Speech
Present Tense	——>	Past Tense
Present Continuous Tense	——>	Past Continuous Tense
Can	——>	Could
Will	——>	Would
May	——>	Might
Must	——>	Had to
Have to	——>	Had to

E X A M P L E :

Present Continuous	Peter: "Maria and I are leaving at six o'clock." Peter announced that <u>they were leaving</u> at six o'clock.
Can	Andrea: "I can speak Italian fluently." Andrea said <u>she could speak</u> Italian fluently.
Will	Vu said, "I will finish the report today." Vu said that he <u>would finish</u> the report today.
May	Meena: "We may not arrive on time." Meena felt that <u>they might not arrive</u> on time.
Must/ Have to	Belita: "I must pay the phone bill before Friday." Belita exclaimed that <u>she had to pay</u> the phone bill before Friday.

PRACTICE 3

Put the following statements into indirect speech.
Use an appropriate reporting verb:

EXAMPLE: **Meena said, "The fire escape is blocked."**
Meena said that the fire escape was blocked.

1. **Juanita:** "I must get my flu *shots* before the winter."

2. **Tam:** "I take lots of Vitamin C in the winter."

3. **Simon:** "I think taking Vitamin C prevents colds."

4. **Meena:** "My doctor doesn't agree with you."

5. **Simon:** "I am trying to exercise more."

6. **Tam:** "*Herbal* medicine can be very good for people."

7. **Meena:** "I swim every day."

8. **Meena:** "Tennis is fun too, but you can't play all year-round."

9. **Simon:** "I'm going to take up cross-country skiing this year."

10. **Tam:** "That sounds like fun."

LET'S FOCUS

DIRECT AND INDIRECT SPEECH: NOTES

1. When putting the <u>imperative voice</u> into indirect speech, change the verb to the infinitive form.

> **E X A M P L E :** **She warned the child, "Do not play with matches."**
> **She warned the child <u>not to play</u> with matches.**
>
> **The boss told Mr. Galetti, "Bend your knees when lifting a heavy object."**
>
> **The boss told Mr. Galetti <u>to bend</u> his knees when lifting a heavy object.**

2. When the verb <u>deny</u> (to say no) is used as a main verb other changes are necessary in the subordinate clause.

> **E X A M P L E :** **The President: "I am not guilty."**
> **The President <u>said he was</u> not guilty.**
> **The President <u>denied that he was</u> guilty.**

3. If the main verb in indirect speech is in the present tense, do not change the tense of the verb in the subordinate clause.

> **E X A M P L E :** **Meena: "I'm leaving work now."**
> **Meena says that <u>she is leaving</u> work now.**

4. In indirect speech <u>that</u> is optional.

> **E X A M P L E :** **Joan said that she was studying hard.**
> **Joan said she was studying hard.**

WORK TOGETHER

Below is a series of pictures and a story to go with the pictures. The story is not in the right order. Work with a partner to decide the correct order of the story, then retell the story using indirect speech.

1. "Please help! There is a fire at my house."

2. "You are very lucky you didn't burn yourself."

3. "Lunch is almost ready."

4. "Timmy, don't ever play with matches. They are dangerous."

5. "Mom, there is a fire in the living room!"

6. "Oh wow! What a great bonfire."

◆ LET'S FOCUS

INDIRECT SPEECH: QUESTIONS

Yes/No Questions

When we use indirect speech to express Yes/No questions, we introduce the subordinate clause with <u>if</u> and change the question form to a statement. No question mark is necessary.

EXAMPLE: **Carla: "Is it raining?"**
Carla <u>asked if it was raining.</u>
Peter: "Can you help me?"
Peter <u>asked if I could help him.</u>

Information Questions (who, what, when, where, why, how)

When we use indirect speech to express information questions, we introduce the subordinate clause with the appropriate question word: what, when, where, etc. We place the verb in the correct tense and change the question order to statement order. We also drop the auxiliary <u>do</u>.

EXAMPLE: **Andrea: "Where is Peter?"**
Andrea <u>asked where Peter was.</u>

EXAMPLE: **Paul: "What are you doing?"**
Paul <u>asked what I was doing</u>.
Meena: "Where do you live?"
Meena <u>asked where I lived</u>.

◇ **Be sure to change the question order to statement order.**

EXAMPLE: **What time is it?**
Correct: He asked what time it was.
Incorrect: He asked what time was it.

74

PRACTICE 4

Change direct speech to indirect speech.

> **E X A M P L E :** **Juan asked: "Can I buy this medicine over the counter in Canada?"**
> **Juan asked if he could buy this medicine over the counter in Canada.**

1. The Nurse to Meena: "Do you have your health card?"

2. Doctor to Bobby: "How are you feeling today?"

3. Peter to Belita: "Do I need a prescription for this medicine?"

4. Pedro to Juanita: "Where is the nearest pharmacy?"

5. Pedro to Pharmacist: "Do you carry ginger tea?"

6. Doctor to Meena: "What seems to be the trouble?"

7. Andrea to Belita: "Are you eating enough fruit and vegetables?"

8. Doctor to Lab Technician: "When will the results of the tests be ready?"

9. Midwife to Sue Yen: "Can you hear the baby's heart beat?

10. Sue Yen to Midwife: "When is the baby due?"

WORK TOGETHER

John hurt his back at work. He read the directions on the poster on the following page. Write down what the poster told the employer to do. Then, with a partner, write down what the poster told John to do.

> **E X A M P L E :** **The poster said that John had to obtain first aid promptly.**

IN ALL CASES OF
INJURY/DISEASE

THE EMPLOYER MUST:

1. Make sure first aid is given immediately.
2. Make sure there is a record of the first aid treatment or any advice given to the worker.
3. Complete and give to the worker the Treatment Memorandum Form 156 if more than first aid treatment or advice is needed.
4. Provide immediate transportation to a hospital, a doctor's office, or the worker's home, if necessary.
5. Pay full wages and benefits for the day or shift on which the injury occurred.

THE WORKER MUST:

1. Promptly obtain first aid.
2. Notify the employer of any injury.
3. Notify the employer of the possible onset of a work-related disease/condition.
4. Choose your own doctor or qualified practitioner. Once you have chosen, you may not change doctors without the Workers' Compensation Board's (WCB) permission.
5. Complete and return all WCB forms promptly.

THE EMPLOYERS' REPORT OF INJURY/DISEASE FORM 7

Form 7 must be completed and sent to the Workers' Compensation Board (WCB) within three days of learning of the accident that causes a worker to: be absent from their regular work; assume lighter duties; earn less than regular pay; obtain health care.

Form 7 must also be completed if eye glasses, dentures and/or artificial appliances were damaged as a result of injuries arising out of and in the course of employment.

WORK TOGETHER

This is a copy of the accident report John filled out.

Date: June 10

Company: ACME Moving

Location of Accident: ACME Mover's Warehouse

Time of Accident: 8:30 a.m.

Description of Accident: John Smith attempted to move a heavy piece of furniture by himself. He dropped it on his foot. His co-worker took him to the hospital. He was referred to his own doctor.

Follow up: ✔ HOSPITAL _____ THERAPY
_____ NURSE ✔ OWN DOCTOR

Submitted by: Mary Casey

Position: Supervisor

"See your own doctor."

"Take 1 week off work."

WORK TOGETHER

Work with a partner. Now look at the cartoon story on the previous page. Then write up an accident report. You may write as Tana, her co-worker, or her supervisor. Use modals and reported speech where possible.

Date:

Company:

Location of Accident:

Time of Accident:

Description of Accident:

Follow up: _____ HOSPITAL _____ THERAPY
_____ NURSE _____ OWN DOCTOR

Submitted by:

Position:

St. John Ambulance

The international voluntary agency, St. John Ambulance, was founded in Canada over 100 years ago. It has helped Canadians to improve their health, safety, and quality of life by providing training and community service. The two groups which make up St. John Ambulance are the Volunteer Brigade and the training department.

The Volunteer Brigade provides first aid services at community events. It is made up of volunteers of all ages. St. John Ambulance acts as designated *backup* in

the event of a large-scale emergency. Members of the Volunteer Brigade wear a black and white uniform.

The training department meets the first aid, CPR, and health care training needs of the community by providing:

◆ training in first aid, CPR, or health care
◆ an on site *Substance Abuse* Prevention Workshop that deals with substance abuse in the workplace
◆ numerous safety-oriented first aid courses

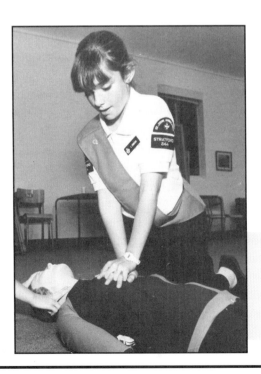

In addition to the Volunteer Brigade and the training department, St. John Ambulance offers courses in family health care, child care, and babysitting.

Comprehension Check

1. When and where was St. John Ambulance founded?

2. What are the two groups that make up the St. John Ambulance?

3. What are some of the services it provides?

ACTIVITY

What are some of the hazards in these scenes?

ACTIVITY

With a partner write some road safety rules:

1. for children
2. for cyclists
3. for motorists
4 for pedestrians

ACTIVITY

Who wears the following protective clothing on the job:

lab coat
gloves
safety shoes
hair net
sound mufflers
seat belt
goggles
mask

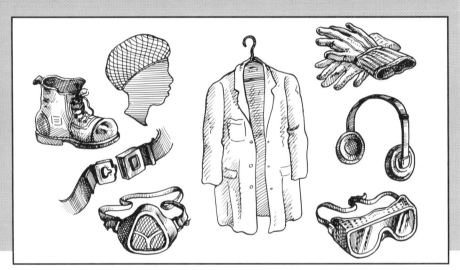

GLOSSARY

backup – extra support

herbal – from a plant

shots – injections

substance abuse – over use of non-prescription drugs or alcohol

IDIOMS

get the hang of it –understand or manage to do something

UNIT

5 MOVING AHEAD

SETTING THE SCENE

1. Where are Mahesh and Claude sitting?

2. What kinds of plans are they making?

Mahesh: Where are you going to study next year?

Claude: I'm going to go to a local community college.
I haven't decided which one yet.

Mahesh: *How come you chose* a college and not a university?

Claude: Well, the universities don't offer the program I'm interested in. Besides the colleges offer more *hands-on* skills training.

Mahesh: What programme are you taking?

Claude: I'm taking the hotel management programme. How about you Mahesh? Where are you going to study next year?

Mahesh: I'm going to attend McGill.

Claude: Are you going to live in *residence*?

Mahesh: Yes, first year is going to be tough. It'll be more convenient if I live on *campus*.

Claude: You'll probably have more fun too, if you live on campus. There are always lots of residence parties.

Mahesh: I won't have much time for parties. I'll have to work really hard to get into medical school.

Claude: I guess you're right.

Mahesh: I'm driving to Montreal next weekend to *check out* the residence. Do you want to come?

Claude: Sure!

Comprehension Check

1. What career is Claude interested in?

2. What career is Mahesh interested in?

3. What are they going to do next weekend?

LET'S FOCUS

THE FUTURE

We use the <u>present continuous</u> to express an action which is sure to happen in the future.

We use the <u>simple present</u> in a similar way to express the future. However, it has a more formal quality.

◇ **Both uses require a time expression.**

Affirmative Statements	**Negative Statements**
She <u>is expecting</u> her first child in August.	They <u>aren't leaving</u> tomorrow.
The Prime Minister <u>leaves</u> for the conference tomorrow.	The tour <u>doesn't begin</u> until after lunch.

Yes/No Questions	**Information Questions**
<u>Is</u> John <u>starting</u> work next week?	What <u>are</u> you <u>doing</u> this weekend?

We use <u>be + going to + verb</u> when we have decided to do something in the future; to express plans or intentions.

Affirmative Statements	**Negative Statements**
I <u>am going to go</u> to college next year.	I'<u>m not going to go</u> to college next year.
She <u>is going to go</u> to college next year.	She <u>isn't going to go</u> to college next year.
We <u>are going to go</u> to college next year.	We <u>aren't going to go</u> to college next year.

Yes/No Questions	**Information Questions**
<u>Are</u> you <u>going to go</u> to college next year?	Which college <u>are</u> you <u>going to go</u> to next year?

LET'S FOCUS

We use the modal <u>will</u> + the simple form of the verb to express a future intention when that intention is not premeditated.

> **E X A M P L E : That's the phone: I'<u>ll</u> get it.**

We also use <u>will</u> for prediction.

> **E X A M P L E : He's late. The store <u>will</u> be closed.**

We use <u>will</u> to make a promise.

> **E X A M P L E : I'<u>ll</u> meet you after school.**

◇ **We can use the negative form of will to express future intention, planned or unplanned.**

E X A M P L E :   **Will not = Won't**

I <u>won't</u> take that course this semester.

I'm not going to take that course this semester.

PRACTICE 1

Complete the following sets of sentences with <u>(be) going to</u> or <u>will</u>. Look carefully at the context.

E X A M P L E : After he graduates, Mahesh <u>is going to</u> (study) medicine.

1. A. I have to study for my statistics exam this weekend.
   B. Don't worry. I____(help) you.

2. A. What_____ you (do) this evening?
   B. I_____(register) for a night school course in computers.

PRACTICE 1

3. A. Juan seems pretty unhappy with his classes. I think he _____ (drop out) sooner or later.

    B. Didn't he tell you? He _____ (start) looking into business courses next week.

4. I think I _____ (take) a math upgrading course next September.

5. I want to register for a Spanish class that starts next week, but I _____ (be able/not) to attend the first class.

6. A. I _____ (turn on) the computer.

    B. Oh, good! When you're finished, I _____ (enter) some data for my project.

7. We need to sign a permission slip so that Bobby can go on a field trip to the museum. I _____ (do) it tomorrow, before I take him to school.

PRACTICE 2

Choose from will, simple present and present continuous to complete the following.

E X A M P L E :   **Hurry! The class <u>starts</u> (start) in five minutes.**

1. We _____ (graduate) this Friday.

2. I _____ (go back) to school some day.

3. The children are working on a chemistry experiment. I hope they _____ not do anything foolish.

PRACTICE 2

4.A. _____ you _____ (see) Tim's teacher soon?

B. Yes, I_____ (meet) him this afternoon to discuss placing Tim in a *gifted class*.

5. School registration_____(begin) next week.

6. We_____(enrol) Marushka in the gifted programme in the fall.

7. She_____(attend) one day a week.

8. _____ she _____ (take) Heritage Language classes as well?

9. Absolutely. She _____(start) in September.

PRACTICE 3

Carla and Andrea are discussing two friends they have in common. Carla has *lost track of* them, so she has many questions to ask Andrea.

Use a variety of forms to express a future meaning in the following dialogue.

Andrea: I ran into Anna and Tracey the other day. They really had lots of news to tell me.

Carla: Oh, I haven't seen them in ages. What have they *been up to*?

Andrea: Let's get a cup of coffee, and I____(tell) you everything. To start with, Anna_____(get) her Master's degree this spring. After she gets her degree, she_____(start) looking for a job at a community college. She'd like to teach up north. That's where she's from originally.

PRACTICE 3

Carla: That's wonderful. What _____ she _____ (do) with her daughter? _____ she take her up north too?

Andrea: Yes, she_____. Anna_____(leave) her with her mother until she finds a job.

Carla: And what about Tracey? What's she doing?

Andrea: Well, Tracey wants to go back to school in the fall. She_____(take) ESL courses all summer to prepare. Then she_____(write) the TOEFL in August.

Carla: That's a hard test, but I'm sure she_____ (do) well.

WORK TOGETHER

How are the many types of educational institutions listed below different? Talk about programs, costs, registration requirements, etc.

1. Colleges
2. Universities
3. *Co-ops*
4. Separate Schools
5. Private Schools
6. Public Schools

WORK TOGETHER

Get a calendar from a local college or university. Plan a course of study in a program you are interested in.

LET'S GET SET

1. Where are Patrick and Michelle?

2. What do you think they are talking about?

EVENING SCHOOL

Michelle: This is going to be an interesting course.

Patrick: I'll try it this evening. But if I don't like it I'm *dropping out.* There are a lot of other things I could be doing.

Michelle: Like what, *vegging out* in front of the TV?

Patrick: What's wrong with that? I work hard all day and I'm entitled to some *R & R.* I don't know why I let you drag me to this class.

Michelle: It's for your own good. You keep talking about opening your own business. This course will give you some important *tips* as well as practical information. Now be quiet. Here comes the teacher.

AFTER CLASS . . .

Patrick: That guy really knows what he's talking about. I can't wait till the next class. Aren't you glad I talked you into coming?

Michelle: Yes, I don't know what I'd do without you.

Comprehension Check

1. Who is more interested in taking the course, Michelle or Patrick?

2. Did Patrick decide to drop the course?

LET'S FOCUS

THE FIRST CONDITIONAL

The first conditional is also called the real or true conditional. We use it to talk about situations that we believe are real or which will probably be real.

> **E X A M P L E :** **<u>If it rains</u>, I will get wet.**
>
> **They will pass the exam <u>if they work hard</u>.**

The <u>if</u> clause may take the simple present, present continuous, or present perfect.

The <u>main</u> clause may take future forms, modals (can, may, might, must), or imperative.

> **E X A M P L E :** **If I <u>save</u> enough money, I <u>can</u> go to UBC.**
>
> **Mahesh <u>is going to go to</u> Med School if he <u>gets</u> accepted.**
>
> **If Patrick <u>has studied</u>, he'<u>ll pass</u> the test.**

◇ **When the <u>if</u> clause comes first, it must be followed by a comma.**
When the <u>main</u> clause comes first, the comma is not necessary.

PRACTICE 4

Complete these sentences:

1. If Mahesh studies math this term, _____.

2. If Claude decides to go to a community college, _____.

3. If I take accounting, _____.

PRACTICE 4

4. I will pass my course if _____.

5. Mahesh can get a *scholarship* if _____.

6. If Frank gets accepted at UBC, _____.

7. If you take communications this term, _____.

8. Claude is going to enrol in modern languages if_____.

9. If Sue wants to upgrade her computer skills, _____.

10. I might *audit* this Canadian History course if _____.

LET'S FOCUS

UNLESS

Unless means <u>if not</u>. It is used in exactly the same way as if.

E X A M P L E : **If I don't study, I won't pass.**

<u>Unless</u> I study, I won't pass.

PRACTICE 5

Change the following <u>if not</u> sentences to <u>unless</u>.

E X A M P L E : **<u>If</u> Mahesh doesn't take calculus, he won't be able to take physics in university.**

<u>Unless</u> Mahesh takes calculus, he won't be able to take physics in University.

PRACTICE 5.

1. If I don't study English now, I may not pass my Engineering exam.

2. We'll be late for class if we don't leave now.

3. Howard speaks six languages if I'm not mistaken.

4. You're going to miss the application deadline if you don't send your forms in soon.

5. Claude doesn't have to take chemistry if he doesn't want to, but his mother thinks he should.

PRACTICE 6

Complete the following sentences.

E X A M P L E : Unless I get a scholarship, I can't go to university.

1. Can I send my child to a different school if_____.

2. If Tam takes too many credits, he _____.

3. Unless Elsa completes her *prerequisite*, the instructor _____.

4. If you drop out of school,_____.

5. If Sue Yen can get day-care for the baby, _____.

6. I have to upgrade my math skills if _____.

7. If your child hasn't been vaccinated for various communicable diseases,_____ before you can enrol her in school.

8. Unless the government stops raising tuition fees, _____.

WORK TOGETHER

With a partner write six questions about the education system in Canada. Use <u>if</u> or <u>unless</u> clauses in your questions.

E X A M P L E : What TOEFL score do I need if I want to go to university?

WORK TOGETHER

Work with a small group to write a list of <u>questions</u> that you would ask in the following situations. Use <u>if</u> clauses in all of your questions.

1. An interview with a school principal.

E X A M P L E : Can you provide tutoring if Bobby is having difficulty with his work?

2. Talking to a college or university's academic counsellor.

3. Talking to an employer about taking courses to upgrade your skills.

ROLE PLAY

Work with a partner or small group. Choose one of the following situations and create a dialogue.

Use as many conditional expressions as you can.

Role Play: Mahesh and Claude will soon be graduating from High School. They are talking about their future plans with a group of friends. One friend thinks she might drop out of school because she has been offered a job in a fashionable clothing store. Role play a possible conversation among the friends.

Role Play: Ting Mei, Peter, and some friends are discussing what Ting Mei should do now that he is in Canada. Ting Mei wants to get a job immediately. Sue Yen thinks he should improve his English first. With your classmates role play a possible conversation.

The Court Watching Program in British Columbia

As you know, the criminal and *civil* court process can be difficult for new Canadians to understand because of language and cultural barriers.

The Law Courts Education Society provides a court watching program for all secondary and ESL students.

The court watching program consists of an orientation to the court system and a list of *criminal* and civil cases for students to observe during their visit. In some cases, arrangements can be made for students to actually meet with court personnel and *judiciary* to learn about their roles in the justice system.

The Law Courts Education Society also has translated materials on the court system in Punjabi, Cantonese, Vietnamese, and Spanish which are available to all students upon request. The purpose of this programming is to link the community with the British Columbia court system and to make the legal process easier to understand for ESL students living in the community.

DISCUSS ◆◆◆◆◆◆◆◆◆◆◆◆◆◆◆◆◆◆◆◆◆◆

1. Why do you think it is important to understand basic laws and regulations in Canada?

2. Would a program, like the court watching program in British Columbia, benefit new Canadians in other provinces?

3. Do you know a lot about the legal system in your country of origin?

GLOSSARY

audit – Attend a class without seeking an official credit

campus – college location

check out – investigate

civil – laws concerning private rights

criminal – laws concerning public safety

co-op programme – a programme in which students work for part of the year and study for the other part

drop out – discontinue studies

gifted class – a class for talented students

hands on – practical training

how come you chose – colloquial for "Why did you choose" *Note:* does not use past tense auxiliary

judiciary – court personnel

lose track of – lose contact with

prerequisite – a necessary course that prepares one for further courses

residence – accommodation on campus

R & R – rest and relaxation

scholarship – award for school fees

tips – helpful hints

to be up to – to be involved in

veg out – relax

UNIT 6
A PLACE OF OUR OWN

SETTING THE SCENE

1. What are Juanita and Pedro looking for in the newspaper?

Juanita: Let's go through the *classifieds*. It's the easiest way to find an apartment.

Pedro: O.K. You take this page and I'll take this one. It'll be quicker.

Juanita: This one sounds good. The rent is only $650 per month for a two bedroom.

Pedro:	The rent is lower than the rent here, but the building is in worse condition than this one.
Juanita:	How do you know that?
Pedro:	I've been there a couple of times. Miguel lives there.
Juanita:	Well how about this one on Main Street? It's only a few *blocks* from the subway, and the rent is more *affordable* than the others listed.
Pedro:	That certainly would be a more *convenient* location than this one.
Juanita:	I've seen that building. It has the best security system I've ever seen. There are video cameras in the lobby, laundry room, recreation room, and the underground garage. They are monitored by a security guard 24 hours a day.
Pedro:	That's a good idea. It's a lot safer than this building.
Juanita:	And it's a lot closer to the subway. Just think! We wouldn't have to get up as early as we do now to go to work. Why don't we go over and have a look at it after work.
Pedro:	Sure!
Juanita:	Good! I'll call and make an appointment.

Comprehension Check

1. Why don't they want to see the apartment for $650 per month?

2. What are the reasons why Juanita and Pedro are going to see the apartment on Main Street?

3. When are they going to see the apartment?

LET'S FOCUS

COMPARATIVE STRUCTURE 1
ADJECTIVES + ER

We use the suffix <u>er</u> and the word <u>than</u> to make the comparative form of adjectives when they have one syllable.

smaller than
bigger than

E X A M P L E : **The new house is big<u>ger</u> <u>than</u> the old house.**

◇ **When the adjective has two syllables and ends in <u>y</u>, change the <u>y</u> to <u>i</u> before adding <u>er</u>.**

easier than
prettier than

E X A M P L E : **This neighbourhood is prett<u>ier</u> than the old neighbourhood.**

◇ **The following words do not follow the rules mentioned above.**

Adjective	Comparative Form
good	better
well	better
bad	worse
badly	worse
far	farther/further

E X A M P L E : **The old car was <u>good</u>, but the new car is <u>better</u>.**

◇ **The word <u>than</u> is omitted when the comparative is not followed by an object.**

E X A M P L E : **This apartment building is older.**

PRACTICE 1

Work in pairs. Use the comparative form of the adjectives provided to complete the sentences.

Juanita: I can't believe this building is only three years old.

Pedro: It certainly looks a lot _____ . (old)

Juanita: That's because it's already *falling apart* and it's usually dirty.

Pedro: I know. The superintendent should keep it _____. (clean)

Juanita: Whenever we turn the heater on it always *makes such a racket*. I wish there was some way to make it _____. (quiet)

Pedro: The *super* promised he would send someone to fix it, but *don't hold your breath*.

Juanita: I guess we shouldn't complain. At least the rent is low.

Pedro: Yeah, and there are a lot of other apartment buildings, with _____ (high) rents, that are in _____(bad) condition.

Juanita: Some of them are even _____ (new) than this one. Oh! I almost forgot to tell you the elevator is out of service.

Pedro: Not again! There's always something wrong with that elevator. I wish they would install a _____ (good) one.

Juanita: Well, soon we won't have to worry about it anymore. Our new place is not only _____ (big) and _____ (nice), it's on the ground floor.

Pedro: You're right! I'm sure we'll be much _____ (happy) there.

PRACTICE 2

Look at the information below about Juanita's and Pedro's present apartment and their old apartment. Write sentences that compare the old apartment to the new one. Use the comparative form of the adjective.

Old Apartment   **New Apartment**

EXAMPLE:

  rent $650/month   rent $800/month

  **Their old apartment is <u>cheaper</u> than their new apartment.
  The rent for their old apartment is <u>lower</u>.**

1. 3 years old   1 year old

2. 30 minutes from subway   5 minutes from subway

3. suite on 16th floor   suite on 1st floor

4. in poor condition   in good condition

5. dark halls   bright halls

6. friendly super   unfriendly super

7. noisy neighbours   quiet neighbours

PRACTICE 3

Work with a partner. Use the following information to make sentences about the differences between the country and the city. Discuss the sentences. Are they true or false?

EXAMPLE: **crime rate/low ... in the country ... in the city
The crime rate in the country <u>is lower than</u> the crime rate in the city.**

PRACTICE 3

1. people/friendly
2. streets/clean
3. houses/far apart
4. traffic/light
5. way of life/healthy

6. evenings/quiet
7. stars/bright
8. goods/cheap
9. air/fresh
10. children/happy

LET'S GET SET

HOUSEWARMING PLANS

1. Why is Michelle calling Sue?

Michelle: Hi Sue! It's Michelle. How are you?

Sue: Oh, hi Michelle! I'm fine thanks. How are you?

Michelle: Fine thanks. I'm calling to invite you to our new house. We're having a *housewarming* on Saturday evening.

Sue: You bought a new house?! That's great! I'd love to come.

Michelle: Good. I'm glad you can make it.

Sue: Tell me all about your new house.

Michelle: Well, it's my *dream house*. It's a lot bigger and more comfortable than the old one. It has four bedrooms and three bathrooms. There's an *ensuite* in the master bedroom, so no more fighting with the kids over the bathroom.

Sue: What's the kitchen like?

Michelle: It's quite big with lots of cupboards and there's a *walkout* to the back porch. There's also a *den*, a main floor laundry room, and a family room.

Sue: It sounds wonderful. What's the neighbourhood like?

Michelle:	It's a really nice, safe neighbourhood. In fact, there's a *Neighbourhood Watch* programme. There are schools, a library, a community centre, and a corner store all within walking distance. The shopping mall is only ten minutes away by car.
Sue:	Have you met any of your neighbours yet?
Michelle:	Yes. We've already met the family next door. I'm sure we're going to love it here. I'll see you next Saturday Sue. *Drop by* around 8 o'clock.
Sue:	See you Saturday Michelle, bye.

Comprehension Check

1. Why is Michelle calling Sue?

2. Did Sue accept Michelle's invitation?

3. Does Michelle like the new house?

LET'S FOCUS

COMPARATIVE STRUCTURE 2
ADJECTIVES AND ADVERBS + MORE AND LESS

The words <u>more</u> and <u>less</u> are used before the adjective or adverb:

1. before most adjectives and adverbs of two or more syllables.
   <u>more</u> beautiful <u>than</u>
   <u>less</u> comfortable <u>than</u>

2. before adverbs that have the suffix <u>ly</u>.
   <u>more</u> fluently <u>than</u>

◇ **The word <u>less</u> is used to express the opposite of <u>more</u>.**

   E x a m p l e : **This house is <u>less</u> expensive <u>than</u> a new one.**

WORK TOGETHER

Work with a partner. Use the following information to compare Michelle's old house and her new house.
Form the comparative with <u>more...than</u> and <u>less...than</u>.

E X A M P L E : **The new house is more spacious than the old house.**

The new neighbourhood has less crime than the old neighbourhood.

Qualities	New House	Old House
Size	3000 sq. feet	1800 sq. feet
Price	$500,000	$285,000
Age	1 year	20 years
Location	suburbs	in town
Neighbourhood	almost no crime	lots of break-ins
Condition	excellent	needs a new roof
Monthly Expenses	$1800	$750
Transportation	only rush hour and no weekend service	frequent subway and bus service 7 days/week

DISCUSS ◆◆◆◆◆◆◆◆◆◆◆◆◆◆◆◆◆◆◆◆◆

1. Do you have programmes in your country of origin like "Neighbourhood Watch"? Do you think they are a good idea? Why or why not?

2. Do you have "housewarmings" in your country? How do you celebrate moving into a new home?

LET'S FOCUS

◇ **We often use repetition in order to show a progressive change or trend.**

1. repeat the comparative adjective for adjectives of one syllable.

   E X A M P L E : **People are living <u>longer</u> and <u>longer</u>.**

2. repeat the qualifier <u>more</u> for adjectives and adverbs of two syllables or more.

   E X A M P L E : **Life in the cities is becoming <u>more</u> and <u>more</u> hectic.**

PRACTICE 4

Complete the following sentences about city life. Repeat the <u>comparative adjective</u> or the qualifier <u>more</u>.

E X A M P L E : **Modern homes are becoming more and more comfortable.**

1. As cities grow they become _____ . (noisy)

2. The cost of living in the city is getting_____ . (expensive)

3. Living in the city has been getting _____ . (bad)

4. Life in the city is becoming_____. (stressful)

5. The cities are becoming _____ (crowded) as more people move into them.

6. City streets have become _____ . (dirty)

LET'S FOCUS

MAKING COMPARISONS WITH AS...AS and NOT AS...AS

When we compare qualities or things that are similar, we use:
<u>as + adj./adv.+ as</u>

Affirmative:

Chantal is <u>as unhappy as</u> Claude about going to a new school.

Negative:

Suzanne isn't <u>as old as</u> Chantal.

Affirmative:

Chantal plays the piano <u>as well as</u> Claude does.

Negative:

Suzanne doesn't play the piano <u>as well as</u> Chantal does.

PRACTICE 5

Write a new sentence which compares the first sentence to the second sentence using "as...as".

E X A M P L E : **Older homes are poorly insulated.**
Modern homes are well insulated.

Older homes are not <u>as well insulated as</u> modern homes.

1. Older homes are well built.
Modern homes are well built.

2. Cottages are very small.
Mansions are very big.

3. Apartments are cheap.
Houses are expensive.

PRACTICE 5

4. House trailers are comfortable.
A traditional house is comfortable.

5. A penthouse suite is very luxurious.
A regular apartment suite is not very luxurious.

DISCUSS ◆◆◆◆◆◆◆◆◆◆◆◆◆◆◆◆◆◆◆◆◆◆◆◆◆

Compare your home in Canada with your home in your country of origin. Include details about size, age, cost, features, and location.

LET'S FOCUS

SUPERLATIVE WITH THE...EST

We use <u>the</u> before the adjective and add the suffix <u>est</u> to one syllable adjectives to form the superlative.

EXAMPLE: Claude is older than Suzanne, but Chantal is <u>the</u> <u>oldest</u>.
(old)

When the adjective has two syllables and ends in <u>y</u>, change the <u>y</u> to <u>i</u> before adding <u>est</u>.

EXAMPLE: Paul never tells any jokes. David sometimes tells jokes.
(funny) Henry always tells jokes. David is funnier than Paul, but Henry is the <u>funniest</u>.

PRACTICE 6

Complete the following sentences with the superlative form of the adjective in parentheses.

EXAMPLE: **The <u>coldest</u> (cold) part of the house is the fruit cellar.**

1. The _____ (big) room in a house is usually the living room.
2. The _____ (high) part of a house is the attic.
3. The _____ (low) part of a house is the basement.
4. The _____ (cozy) room in a house is usually the kitchen.
5. The _____ (messy) part of a house is often the closets.

LET'S FOCUS

SUPERLATIVE WITH THE MOST...

The words <u>the most</u> are used to form the superlative before adverbs and adjectives of more than two syllables.

EXAMPLE: **<u>The most beautiful</u> view of the city is from the top of the tower.**

PRACTICE 7

Complete these sentences with the appropriate superlative form of the adjective provided.

1. Apartments are _____ (common) type of accommodation for people who live in the city.
2. Three bedroom homes seem to be _____ (popular) size family home.

PRACTICE

3. The Prime Minister's address, 24 Sussex Dr., is _____ (famous) address in Canada.

4. The _____ (dangerous) luxury feature in a home with children is the swimming pool.

PRACTICE 8

HOMES

Different Housing for Different Tastes!

Call Your Sales Representative

Most people in Canada live in traditional homes such as a house or an apartment. However, there are a number of people who live in non-traditional homes. Some examples of non-traditional homes are: cabins, nursing homes, boarding houses, rooming houses, trailers, boats, residences (dormitories), group homes, and mansions. Some of these homes are in isolated areas and have no modern conveniences, while others have every modern convenience.

Weekend Retreat!

Rustic Log Cabin, with lake view.
Backs onto trees.

Why Rent?

Just listed! Super clean 8 yr. old trailer home.
Two bedrooms, all furnished, priced to go!

What a Deal!

Ground floor Apartment. Walkout to patio.
Great for seniors.

PRACTICE 8

Work in small groups and discuss the types of homes mentioned on the previous page. For each type of home answer the following questions.

What kind of home is it?
What special features does it have?
Does this type of home exist in other countries?
Who lives there?
Why do they live there?

WORK TOGETHER

In groups of three or four use the classified ads in your local newspaper to choose the most appropriate home for each of the following:

1. newlyweds on a small budget
2. a single business executive
3. senior citizens on a fixed income
4. four college students

Give reasons why you chose the homes you did.

ROLE PLAY

1. A couple house-hunting and an aggressive real estate salesperson.
2. A tenant complaining to the landlord about something which needs repairing.
3. It's late in the evening. The people in the next apartment are making a lot of noise. Speak to your neighbours about the noise.
4. A landlord telling tenants about *fumigating* the apartment.
5. Make small talk with your neighbour: in the elevator, in the laundry room, at the bus stop.

WORK TOGETHER

In pairs or small groups design your own home.
Use the comparative and superlative forms to talk about its features, location and size. Include information about the neighbourhood or location.

WRITE ABOUT YOURSELF

Compare your dream house or apartment to Michelle's dream house.

ACTIVITY

Match the words in column A with the appropriate definition in column B.

A	B
1. solarium	**a.** room directly under the roof
2. bungalow	**b.** unheated room in basement
3. basement	**c.** payment for use of land or building
4. fruit cellar	**d.** bathroom in master bedroom
5. mortgage	**e.** glass enclosed room
6. ensuite	**f.** place for sitting outside house
7. semi-detached	**g.** room of building below ground level
8. attic	**h.** house with only one floor
9. rent	**i.** house which is attached to another house
10. porch	**j.** property as security for a loan

FIGURE IT OUT

Unscramble the following words. Then put the letters in brackets together to reveal the popular saying.

1. LMSROUIA   _ _ [_] _ _ [_]
2. AMORONDLURY   _ [_] [_] _ _ _ _ _ _
3. CSETSARIA   [_] _ _ _ _ _ _ _
4. GHNOSURAWMIE [_][_] _ _ _ _ [_] _ _
5. SENTUIE   [_] _ _ [_] _ _
6. RRNSUYE   _ _ [_] _ _ _
7. HKTICNE   _ _ _ _ [_] _ _
8. WYDRAVIE   _ _ [_] _ _ _ _
9. AUNAS   [_] _ _ _ _
10. HPOCR   _ _ [_]
11. CATIT   [_] _ _ _ _
12. BLSATE   [_][_] _ [_][_]

○ ○○○'○ ○○○○ ○○ ○○○ ○○○○○○

ACTIVITY

A. Complete these very common idioms of comparison with the appropriate adjective. Do you have similar expressions in your language?

quick	old	sick	quiet	light
busy	slow	cute	blind	weak

1. As _____ as a feather   6. As _____ as a mouse
2. As _____ as a beaver   7. As _____ as a bat
3. As _____ as a button   8. As _____ as a dog
4 As _____ as molasses   9. As _____ as a kitten
5. As _____ as a wink   10. As _____ as the hills

B. Now try to complete these idioms of comparison with the appropriate noun.

church mouse	bird	picture	sugar	whistle
pie	ghost	pancake	peacock	lark

1. As happy as a _____
2. As clean as a _____
3. As pale as a _____
4. As easy as _____
5. As poor as a _____
6. As free as a _____
7. As pretty as a _____
8. As sweet as _____
9. As flat as a _____
10. As proud as a _____

GLOSSARY

affordable – at a good price

block – area enclosed by intersecting streets

classifieds – section of newspaper featuring homes for sale, apartments for rent, jobs available, and items for sale

convenient – well suited for one's purpose

den – room in a house or apartment used as an office

dream house – someone's perfect house

ensuite – a two-piece bathroom in a master bedroom

fumigate – spray for insects

housewarming – a party to celebrate moving into a new home

Neighbourhood Watch – a special security programme in many neighbourhoods. People in the community try to keep it safe by watching for suspicious activity and reporting it

walkout – an exit to an outside patio from a room such as a kitchen or family room

IDIOMS

don't hold your breath – don't expect anything to happen

drop by – make a casual visit

falling apart – in poor condition

make a racket – make a lot of noise

super – expression for superintendent

ANSWERS TO FIGURE IT OUT

1. S O L **A** R I U **M**
2. L **A** U **N** D R Y R O O M
3. **S** T A I R C A S E
4. **H O** U S E W A R **M** I N G
5. **E** N S U **I** T E
6. N U R **S** E R Y

7. K I T C **H** E N
8. D R **I** V E W A Y
9. **S** A U N A
10. P O R **C** H
11. **A** T T I C
12. **S** **T** A B **L** **E**

A **M A N** ' **S** **H O M E** **I S** **H I S** **C A S T L E**

ANSWERS FOR ACTIVITY

A.

1. light
2. busy
3. cute
4. slow
5. quick
6. quiet
7. blind
8. sick
9. weak
10. old

B.

1. lark
2. whistle
3. ghost
4. pie
5. church mouse
6. bird
7. picture
8. sugar
9. pancake
10. peacock

UNIT 7

JUST FOR FUN

SETTING THE SCENE

1. Where are Peter, Simon, Belita, and Meena?

2. What do you think they are talking about?

Peter: That was a great movie!

Simon: Yeah, I love watching *action* films.
Hey look! There's Meena and Belita. Hi Meena. Hi Belita.
What movie did you two see?

Meena: We were looking forward to seeing that new *thriller*, but it was *sold out.* The guy at the ticket booth recommended seeing the new Michael J. Fox film.

Simon: How was it?

Belita: It was very funny. I bet you two went to see the action film.

Peter: How did you know?

Belita: You two never miss going to those types of films.

Peter: We'd enjoy seeing that new thriller too. How about seeing it with us next week.

Simon: Sure, we could go next Tuesday.

Belita: That's fine with me. What about you Meena?

Meena: That's fine with me too.

Peter: It's a date then.

Comprehension Check

1. What type of film did Meena and Belita see?

2. What type of film were Meena and Belita looking forward to seeing?

3. What type of film did Simon and Peter see?

LET'S FOCUS

GERUNDS

A gerund is the <u>ing</u> form of the verb <u>functioning as a noun</u>.
Gerunds are used in the following ways in English:

1. as the subject or complement of a sentence.

    E X A M P L E :   **<u>Dancing</u> is fun.**
                        No <u>smoking</u>.
                        His favourite sport is <u>surfing</u>.

2. as the object of the preposition.

    E X A M P L E :   **He is thinking of <u>playing</u> hockey this winter.**

3. after certain phrasal verbs completed by <u>to</u>.

    E X A M P L E :   **I am accustomed to <u>walking</u> long distances.**
                        I am used to <u>waking</u> up early.
                        We look forward to <u>meeting</u> your friend.

4. after the following common verbs.

LIST 1

admit	enjoy	recall
anticipate	finish	recommend
appreciate	can't help	resent
avoid	keep (on)	resist
complete	mention	risk
consider	mind	suggest
delay	miss	talk about
deny	postpone	tolerate
discuss	practise	understand
look forward to	feel like	

◇ **When forming the gerund of a verb ending in <u>e</u> drop the final <u>e</u> but do not double the final consonant.**
E X A M P L E : write -> writing   dance-> dancing

PRACTICE 1

Use a gerund to complete the following sentences.

EXAMPLE: **<u>Swimming</u> is good exercise. I do 50 laps a day.**

1. I'm used to _____ to work. I used to live very near my office. Now I have to go to a gym to work out.

2. My husband is a *couch potato*. He avoids _____.

3. John is afraid of _____ his contact lenses when he goes swimming.

4. _____ video games can be *hypnotic*.

5. How about _____ a movie tonight?

6. Paul won't go hang gliding with us. He can't help _____ afraid of heights.

7. Have you finished _____ your suitcase for the holiday?

8. If you practise figure _____, you'll be as good as Elvis Stojko.

WORK TOGETHER

Work in pairs. Follow the example and ask and answer the following questions using the following verbs. Remember to put the second verb in the gerund form.

Tell me something you _____ in your spare time.

EXAMPLE: **<u>enjoy</u>**
A: Tell me something you <u>enjoy doing</u> in your spare time.
B: I <u>enjoy gardening</u>.

1. avoid
2. don't mind
3. miss
4. resent
5. talk about
6. appreciate
7. look forward to
8. resist
9. never feel like

WORK TOGETHER

Look at the entertainment section of your local newspaper. What are the different ratings or classifications for movies? With your partner find the classification for movies suitable for children; suitable for young people accompanied by an adult; suitable for adults.

Are there other warnings beside the letter classifications?

What do you think they mean?

Why might a movie be classified as "R"?

WORK TOGETHER

Procedure for Conducting a Survey:

Step 1. Work with a partner. Ask the questions on the survey and record his/her responses.

Step 2. Form two Groups: <u>Group A</u> with students who interviewed females and <u>Group B</u> with students who interviewed males.

Step 3. Each group now tabulates survey responses. Record the number of females/males who answered YES to each question. Then record the number of males/females who responded NO to each question.

Participant: **Male** ☐   **Female** ☐

1. What is your favourite type of film?

ACTION/ADVENTURE ☐	DOCUMENTARY ☐	ROMANCE ☐
ANIMATED ☐	FANTASY ☐	SCIENCE FICTION ☐
COMEDY ☐	HORROR ☐	THRILLER ☐
DRAMA ☐	MUSICAL ☐	

2. Do you go to see films because of the:

	YES	NO
ACTORS?	☐	☐
STORY?	☐	☐
DIRECTOR?	☐	☐

118

WORK TOGETHER

		YES	NO
3.	Do you think there is too much censorship?	☐	☐
4.	Do you think there should be more censorship?	☐	☐
5.	Do you think there should be less censorship?	☐	☐
6.	Do you think going to the cinema is too expensive?	☐	☐
7.	Is the quality of films improving?	☐	☐
8.	Is the quality of films declining?	☐	☐
9.	Do you go to see a new film as soon as it opens?	☐	☐
10.	Do you go to see more than 5 movies a month at the cinema?	☐	☐
11.	Do you only go to see films that get good reviews?	☐	☐
12.	Do you wait until a film is on video before you see it?	☐	☐
13.	Do you prefer to rent movies on video?	☐	☐
14.	Do you buy movie videos?	☐	☐

Step 4. As a class, compare and analyze results of the survey.

What did you learn about the average moviegoer in your class?

E X A M P L E :   **Do men and women differ in their viewing habits?**

How many people prefer to rent movies on video?

What do most people think about censorship?

What do most people think about the cost of going to the cinema?

What do most people think about the quality of films today?

LET'S GET SET

1. Where are Andrea and Steve?

2. What are they talking about?

AT THE GAME

Andrea:	I only agreed to come to the football game because you promised to get good tickets.
Steve:	I know I did, but *something came up*. I forgot to call the box office. When I finally remembered to call, these were the only seats they had left.
Andrea:	Well I'm glad I decided to bring my binoculars.
Steve:	You didn't really need to bring them. You can see everything on the giant screen.
Andrea:	I'm thirsty. Would you get me something to drink?
Steve:	Sure.

LATER . . .

Steve:	Here's your drink. I had to wait for a while, and I really hate waiting in line.
Andrea:	Did you remember to get me a straw?
Steve:	No, I'm sorry...but I'm not planning to go back to that line-up. Did anything interesting happen while I was gone?
Andrea:	Not really. The Roughriders got a *touchdown*.

Comprehension Check

1. Is Andrea happy with the seats Steve got for the game?

2. Did Steve bring Andrea a straw for her drink?

LET'S FOCUS

VERBS FOLLOWED BY INFINITIVES

Infinitives have many uses in English:

1. as the subject or complement of a verb.

> **E X A M P L E :** **To swim is difficult. (This sounds very formal.)**
> **It is rewarding to learn a new language.**

2. after certain verbs, many of which involve making plans.

LIST 2

can/can't	afford	forget	promise
	agree	hope	refuse
	appear	learn	seem
	arrange	offer	want
	decide	pretend	would like
	demand	plan	
	expect	need	

PRACTICE 2

Complete the following sentences with any appropriate verb in the infinitive form.

E X A M P L E : **He forgot <u>to buy</u> his season pass this year.**

1. We can't afford _____ a holiday this year.

2. It is wonderful _____ you again.

3. Jane promised _____ reservations for the play.

PRACTICE 2

4. They wanted _____ French before going on holiday.

5. Mahesh plans _____ his relatives in New Delhi after he graduates.

6. The children pretended _____ travellers from outer space.

7. We arranged _____ outside the movie theatre.

8. Paula would like _____ a trip across Canada but her husband wants _____ home on their vacation.

9. One of the most famous quotes from a Shakespearean play is: "_____ or _____. That is the question!"

PRACTICE 3

Work together. Ask and answer questions about what you plan, want, need, would like, or can't afford to do this weekend.

E X A M P L E : **What do you need to do on Saturday?**
I need to go to the nursery to buy
some topsoil for the garden.

ROLE PLAY

Juanita and Pedro would like to take a short trip this weekend to get to know their new province better. What are some interesting places they could visit? Role play a discussion about a short excursion between Juanita, Pedro, and their friends.

LET'S FOCUS

VERBS THAT TAKE A PRONOUN + THE INFINITIVE

Certain verbs express a meaning which causes another person or thing to perform a second action. When a verb follows a verb in this way, the structure is <u>verb + pronoun + infinitive</u>.

E X A M P L E :   She <u>told me to come</u> to the party.
He <u>taught them to ski</u>.
He <u>urged them to drive</u> carefully.

LIST 3

advise	forbid	like	request	urge
allow	force	need	require	want
ask	got	order	teach	warn
cause	help	permit	tell	would like
encourage	instruct	persuade		
expect	invite	remind		

PRACTICE 4

Here is a brochure for a new fitness centre. Complete the blanks using the words from the side of the page.
Use the correct form of the verb.

GRAND OPENING

VERB LIST	Mickey's Fitness Centre
Get Started	Do you want_____ weight and_____ ?
Swim	Do you avoid_____ ?

PRACTICE 4

Join

Help

Lose

Exercise

Use

Shape Up

Work Out

Cycle

Let our experienced staff help you_____ on an aerobics program.

We will teach you_____ our weight lifting equipment.

Do you enjoy _____ and _____ ? We have the facilities!

Our staff will encourage you _____ regularly.

Allow us _____ you become healthier. We urge you _____ today.

LET'S FOCUS

VERBS THAT TAKE THE GERUND OR THE INFINITIVE

Some verbs in English can be followed by either the <u>gerund</u> or <u>infinitive</u> form of the completing verb. The meaning remains the same for the gerund and infinitive forms.

EXAMPLE: I really like sewing/to sew.

LIST 4

begin	continue	like
can't stand	hate	start

PRACTICE 5

Meena, Carla, and Andrea are trying to decide what to do this evening. Since Meena is a new roomate, Carla and Andrea want to find out what she likes to do. Meena enjoys many active sports but she doesn't like playing cards.

With your partner make a list of possible questions for Andrea and Carla and answers for Meena. Use the verbs from list 4.

EXAMPLE: **Do you like playing badminton?**
No, I hate to play racquet sports.

 ## LET'S FOCUS

STOP

There are a limited number of verbs in English that take both the gerund and the infinitive form with each having a <u>different</u> meaning.

When <u>stop</u> is followed by a <u>gerund</u>, the action expressed in the gerund form is being stopped.

EXAMPLE: **I <u>stopped smoking</u> last year.
(I don't smoke anymore.)**

When <u>stop</u> is followed by an <u>infinitive</u>, some action is being stopped in order to perform the action expressed in the infinitive.

EXAMPLE: **I was getting very tired, so I <u>stopped
to have</u> a stretch. (I took a break.)**

PRACTICE 6

Complete the sentences with either the infinitive or gerund. Pay attention to the meaning.

1. You must stop _____ (smoke) if you want _____ (stay) healthy.

2. Please stop _____ (see) me if you are ever in the neighbourhood.

3. Let's stop _____ (watch) so much TV and start _____ (play) badminton instead.

4. They were playing tennis and stopped _____ (drink) some water.

◆ LET'S FOCUS

REMEMBER AND FORGET

When <u>remember</u> or <u>forget</u> is followed by a <u>gerund</u>, the action of remembering occurs <u>after</u> the action expressed in the gerund.

EXAMPLE: **I <u>remember turning off</u> the stove before I left the house.**
(I remember now that I turned off the stove.)

When <u>remember</u> or <u>forget</u> is followed by an <u>infinitive</u>, the action of remembering occurs <u>before</u> the action expressed in the infinitive.

EXAMPLE: **I <u>remembered to turn off</u> the stove before I left the house.**
(I remembered first, then turned off the stove.)

PRACTICE 7

Complete the sentences with either the infinitive or gerund. Pay attention to the meaning.

1. John was sure he remembered _____ (lock) the front door. When he got home from the movie it was open so he called the police.
2. We must remember _____ (see) the doctor about shots for our vacation.
3. Bogdana remembered _____ (make) reservations for the play so they would have good seats.
4. Please remember _____ (meet) me at the tennis courts at 5 o'clock.
5. This time I remembered _____ (buy) the suntan lotion before the holiday.
6. He forgot _____ (see) the film before until the ending.
7. They always forget _____ (cancel) their newspaper when they go on holiday.

LET'S FOCUS

 TRY

When <u>try</u> is followed by a <u>gerund</u>, the action expressed in the gerund usually indicates one of many actions taken.

E X A M P L E : **I couldn't sleep last night. I <u>tried reading</u>, <u>drinking</u> milk, and even <u>exercising</u>. But nothing helped.**

<u>Try</u> followed by an <u>infinitive</u> indicates that the action expressed by the infinitive was attempted—usually unsuccessfully.

E X A M P L E : **I <u>tried to open</u> the window, but it was stuck.**

PRACTICE 8

Complete the sentences with either the infinitive or gerund. Pay attention to the meaning.

1. Each time he got up to bat he tried _____ (hit) the ball.
2. She tried everything _____ (stop) her hiccups. She even tried _____ (stand) on her head.
3. Have you tried _____ (hang-glide). It's so thrilling.
4. I always try _____ (keep up) with current affairs.

Lacrosse

Lacrosse is the oldest organized sport in North America and it is Canada's official summer game. Lacrosse has been played in North America since the 1600s. The Algonquin nations of the St. Lawrence were the first to develop and play the game.

The first peoples called the game *baggataway*. Lacrosse was more than a game. It was also a religious rite and physical training for warriors. Matches sometimes lasted for two to three days. In 1636 a Jesuit missionary gave the game a new name. He called it Lacrosse because the stick used in the game reminded him of a bishop's crozier or "crosse." In 1860, a Montreal dental surgeon, William George Beers, set out standard rules for the game. In 1867, Beers organized the National Lacrosse Association. This helped to spread the game to the United States and Britain.

At the 1978 Commonwealth Games in Edmonton, Canada, as host country, introduced lacrosse to the competition as the new sport. Although sticks made of plastic/aluminum are becoming more popular, the vast majority of wooden lacrosse sticks are still made in North America by Native Peoples.

Comprehension check

1. How did Lacrosse get its name?

2. Who developed the game?

3. When did it become popular in the United States and Britain? Why?

4. Where are the majority of wooden sticks made and by whom?

WORK TOGETHER

With your partner talk about the most popular sport in your country of origin. Do you enjoy playing this sport or do you prefer watching it?

Are men and women equally encouraged to participate in sports in your country?

Are there certain sports men or women shouldn't play?

Maybe you don't like to take part in sports but enjoy using your hands to create different crafts. Talk about popular arts and crafts too.

WORK TOGETHER

In small groups develop a new sport. Make sketches. Remember to include the following:

1. equipment

2. number of players on a team

3. playing area (indoor/outdoor)

4. rules (for play and scoring)

ACTIVITY

Match the person in column A with his/her action in column B

 A

 B

1. A procrastinator prefers...
2. A miser hates...
3. A gossip enjoys...
4. A chatterbox loves
5. A bibliophile likes
6. A couch potato avoids...
7. A philatelist enjoys...
8. A backseat driver likes ...
9. An optimist prefers...
10. A movie buff enjoys...

... talking about other people
... to look at the bright side
... telling the driver how to drive
... to spend money
... to talk
... collecting stamps
... moving from a comfortable couch
... watching films
... to put things off until later
... to read books

GLOSSARY

action film – a film filled with stunts and action

thriller – a film that is filled with suspense and is often frightening

hypnotic – something that holds someone's attention and controls them

touchdown – football score which is obtained by being in possession of the ball behind the opponents' goal line

IDIOMS

sold out – all items which were available for sale have been sold

something came up – something happened unexpectedly and caused a change in plans

couch potato – a person who prefers to sit in front of the TV for many hours at a time, eats junk food, and avoids physical exercise

UNIT

8

SHOPPING AROUND

SETTING THE SCENE

1. What does Pedro want to do on his way to the soccer game?

Pedro: Let's get off at this stop. I need to get some money and there's a bank machine near here.

Ricardo: Those bank machines are great. You can do your banking almost anytime you want.

Pedro: Oh no! I can't remember my *PIN* number. I'll have to go into the bank after all.

Ricardo: While you're getting your cash, I'll look at their *RRSP* rates. We'll have to hurry because the game starts in fifteen minutes.

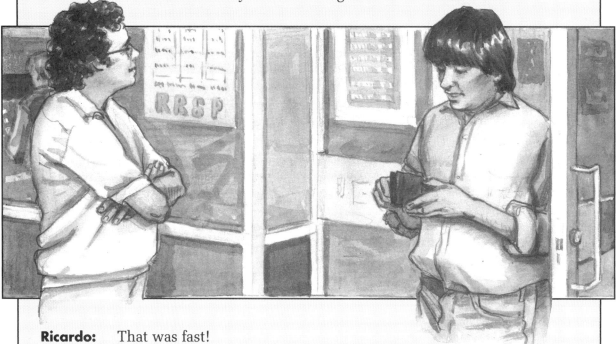

Ricardo: That was fast!

Pedro: The bank was almost empty, so I was able to *withdraw* some money and pay a few bills.

Ricardo: Well, if we hurry, we'll get to the stadium before the game starts.

Comprehension Check

1. Why does Pedro want to use the bank machine?

2. Why can't he use the bank machine?

3. What does Ricardo do while Pedro goes into the bank?

4. Was the bank crowded?

LET'S FOCUS

NON-SEPARABLE PHRASAL VERBS

English contains many phrasal or two-word verbs that have idiomatic meanings.

<u>Get over</u> can mean to climb over an obstacle.

> **E X A M P L E :**   **The fence is too high. I can't <u>get over</u> it.**

But it also means to recover either physically or emotionally.

> **E X A M P L E :**   **The baby is <u>getting over</u> a cold.**
> **Paul never <u>got over</u> his divorce.**

Some of these two-word verbs are non-separable. That means the object of the preposition, whether it is a noun or pronoun, cannot come between the verb and the preposition.

> **E X A M P L E :**   **He <u>got into</u> the taxi.**
> **He <u>got into</u> it.**

PRACTICE 1

Look at the list of non-separable phrasal verbs. Working with a partner, write down all the meanings that you know. Do some of the phrasal verbs have more than one meaning? Check your meanings with another group or ask your instructor if they are correct, after you have completed the exercise. Do not use a dictionary unless you have a dictionary of phrasal verbs.

LIST 1

apply for	fool around with	get through (with)	run out of
ask for	get along (with)	grow up (in)	shop around
call for	get into	listen to	take off
call on	get off	look at	think about
drop out	get out of	look out for	wait for
finish with	get over	run into	watch out for

PRACTICE 2

Using the verbs from list 1 on the previous page complete the following sentences. Use the correct tense of the verb.

EXAMPLE: Paul <u>got off</u> the bus at the wrong stop.

1.   When does the plane _____?

2.   What did you do last night? I _____ music all evening.

3.   When we were on holiday in Mexico, we _____ some old friends. What a coincidence!

4.   I don't _____ him. We disagree about a lot of things.

5. A. I'll meet you outside the movie theatre.
   B. O.K. but please be on time. I _____ (not) you forever.

6.   Oh dear! Simon's coming over this evening and we _____ _____ pop.

7.   Here are Brenda and Joe. I don't believe it! They always _____ _____ us without calling first.

8. A. We're going to Canada's Wonderland.
   B. Have a good time, but _____ that new ride. It's really scary.

9. A. I think the VCR is broken. Hand me a screwdriver so I can take it apart.
   B. Oh don't _____ it. I'll take it to a repair shop.

10.   Did Paul _____ at Calgary or Regina?

WORK TOGETHER

Carla visited friends in another city last weekend. Look at the pictures and talk about different things she and her friends did.

LET'S GET SET

1. Where are Michelle and Monica?
2. What are they doing?

Michelle: My *feet are killing me.* I've got to take my shoes off. I think we went into every store in the mall. I still haven't picked up my dry cleaning yet.

Monica: We can pick it up just before we leave. I probably tried on 15 dresses before I found the right one. Why don't you put on the new running shoes you bought?

Michelle: That's a good idea. I might as well break them in. All the sales people who waited on us were very helpful. They actually tried to help us pick out exactly what we wanted.

Monica: Oh remind me to go to the library before we leave. Mahesh asked me to drop off some CD's.

Michelle: There's a coffee shop. Let's take a break and *recharge our batteries.*

Monica: You were really serious when you said we were going to *shop 'til we dropped.*

Comprehension Check

1. What's wrong with Michelle?

2. What have Michelle and Monica been doing?

3. What does Monica suggest?

4. What must Monica remember to do before they leave the mall?

LET'S FOCUS

SEPARABLE PHRASAL VERBS

Most phrasal verbs are separable. The object of the preposition can be placed between the verb and the preposition.

E X A M P L E : **John called. Please <u>call him back</u>.**
Oh, I <u>called John back</u> already.
You must mean someone else.

◇ **When using a pronoun with separable phrasal verbs, the pronoun <u>must</u> be placed between the verb and the preposition.**

LIST 2

ask out	hand in	put off	tear up
call back	hand out	put on	throw away
call off	hang up	put out	throw out
call up	leave out	shut off	try on
cross out	look over	start over	turn off
do over	look up	take back	turn on
figure out	make up	take off	turn up
fill in	pay back	take out	wake up
fill out	pick up	talk over	write down
fill up	put away	tear down	
find out	put back	tear off	
give back	put down	tear out of	

PRACTICE 3

Below is a list of separable phrasal verbs and their more formal definitions. Working with a partner match up the verbs in Column A with the appropriate one-word definitions in Column B. You may find more than one phrasal verb for the same definition.

Write your verbs and definitions on a separate piece of paper.

A	B
put off	omit
turn down	discard
hand in	cancel
take off	distribute
fill in	discover
leave out	remove
call off	postpone
hand out	refuse
find out	submit
fill out	return
throw out	complete
put back	belittle
take back	insult
put down	
throw away	

Do you know the meanings of the other verbs on list 2?
Check with your partner.

PRACTICE 4

Using the verbs from list 2 fill in the blanks in the following sentences.
Use the correct form of the verb.

EXAMPLE: **This word is difficult to pronounce.
Please <u>look it up</u> in your dictionary.**

1. A. I want to get a credit card.
   B. Please _____ this application.

2. Did you remember _____ the water before we left on our trip?

3. Mary wants me _____ at the subway station.

4. Peter lent me money to pay for dinner the other night. I have to
_____.

5. There is no smoking in the mall. Please _____ your cigarette _____.

6. The plot for the movie was just fantastic. How does the author
_____ these things _____?

7. Claude, your music is too loud. Please _____.

8. I hope it doesn't rain. We had to _____ the picnic last week.
I don't want to do it again.

9. A. These clothes are too small for you.
   B. Should I _____?
   C. No. Let's _____ in the attic until your brother is bigger.
   Then he can wear them and I won't have to buy new ones.

WORK TOGETHER

What are some things you can do at the mall? Using phrasal verbs make up sentences about the things you can do at a mall.

E X A M P L E : **dry cleaner**
You can drop off clothes at the dry cleaner's.

1. the bank
2. photofinishing store
3. supermarket
4. bookstore

5. department store
6. travel agency
7. cinema
8. pharmacy

PRACTICE 5

Sunil and Monica Sharma are going to open up a new bank account and apply for a credit card. Using appropriate verbs from the lists of separable and non-separable phrasal verbs complete the following dialogue. Use the correct tense of the verbs.

Monica: I really think it's time we spoke to the bank about changing our account. All we have is a savings account.
It is very inconvenient. I can't write cheques to pay the bills or anything.

Sunil: Well let's _____ it _____ and decide what kind of account would be better. After all, we get higher interest with a savings account.

Monica: Yes, but the bank charges us a penalty fee everytime I take money out of the savings account.
I've _____ _____ what we need.
We should have a joint account.

PRACTICE 5

Sunil: A joint account! So I can put money in and you can_____ it _____?!

Monica: I work too. Besides, a joint account will be more efficient for paying household bills. It should be a chequing account and I think we should have a new convenience card.

Sunil: What's a convenience card?

Monica: That's a new card that let's me pay at the supermarket without cash. The money is deducted directly from our bank account. I can use it in other stores too.

Sunil: O.K. That's enough. I'm _____ _____ this discussion. I'm not going to _____ _____ these kinds of ideas. I refuse to get one of those new-fangled cards.

Monica: We are _____ _____ in a new country. Some things are going to seem strange at first but I think it's a good idea. Now you should visit the banks and _____ _____ more about these different accounts and what kind of service charges the banks have.

Sunil: O.K. and while I'm there I guess I'll _____ _____ an application form.

Monica: That's the spirit! We'll _____ the form _____ at home. I can concentrate better and Mahesh can help us. We should probably _____ _____ a small loan too.

Sunil: _____ _____ a loan! We don't owe any money. What do we need a loan for?

Monica: I've been _____ _____ this credit information. It says taking out a small loan and then _____ it _____ very quickly is a good way to establish a credit rating.

DISCUSS ◆◆◆◆◆◆◆◆◆◆◆◆◆◆◆◆◆◆◆◆◆◆◆

What do you think about credit cards and convenience cards?

Do you use them? How often?

Trouble At the Local Mall

S MITH FALLS - Local shopkeepers have clashed with teenagers *hanging out* at the uptown mall. Store owners claim teenagers are hanging out at the mall to be with their friends. They try on expensive items like leather jackets or boots without really intending to buy them. This annoys many salespeople because they feel the teens are wasting their time. Shopkeepers also worry that the teenagers might try to shoplift some of the items.

The local teens claim they aren't hurting anyone.

Their parents point out that the teenagers really have nowhere else to go and feel the teens are safer in the mall than out on the street.

WORK TOGETHER

Work in small groups. Half the group should take the side of the teenagers and come up with as many reasons as possible for being allowed to meet in malls.

The other half of the group should take the side of the shopkeepers and come up with reasons to forbid the teenagers from coming to the mall except to make a purchase. Then exchange your ideas.

Possible questions:

Are malls public or private property?

Can you think of any alternative solutions to the problem?

The West Edmonton Mall

West Edmonton Mall

If your first question about a holiday destination is about the shops, the West Edmonton Mall is a dream come true. It is the largest mall in North America. Imagine a mall with 800 stores, 110 restaurants, the largest indoor amusement park, an NHL size hockey rink, the world's largest indoor waterpark, submarine rides, and an eighteen hole golf course.

This megamall is equivalent in size to 48 city blocks and attracts visitors from all over the world. It is not just a place to pop into if you run out of something. It's an entire world unto itself. Enjoy a tropical atmosphere, slides, wild surf and six-foot waves at the World Waterpark. Other amusements include swimming, surfing, suntanning, and *kayaking*.

At the Deep-Sea Adventure go beneath the mall to the Great Barrier Reef in one of four authentic submarines. See exotic fish, bottlenose dolphins, sharks, barracudas, sunken treasure, and a hand-carved replica of Christopher Columbus' *Santa Maria*. Take a course in scuba diving or underwater photography.

Choose from dozens of rides and attractions at the 400,000 square-foot Amusement Park, including "the Mindbender" the world's largest triple-loop roller coaster. Enjoy bumper cars, a Ferris wheel, a hand-carved carousel, a petting zoo, and a huge electric train.

The restaurants feature gourmet cuisine from around the world.

Stroll down a replica of the Bourbon Street in New Orleans, offering thirteen bars and restaurants for evening entertainment or Europa Boulevard modelled after a typical European street.

Art lovers can see rare pieces such as priceless vases from the Ching Dynasty and a valuable solid ivory, hand-carved pagoda from the Ming Dynasty. Replicas of the Crown Jewels of the British Empire from William I to George VI are on display.

The Fantasyland Hotel offers rooms in colorful themes such as the Roman Room reminiscent of the period of Anthony and Cleopatra, Polynesian, Victorian Coach, Truck, and others.

The West Edmonton Mall, the city under one roof, is packed with entertainment and activities for all ages.

Comprehension Check

1. Is the West Edmonton Mall the biggest mall in the world?
2. How many stores and restaurants does it have?
3. What sport can be played there?
4. What are some things you can you do at the mall?

WORK TOGETHER

Male Shoppers Versus Female Shoppers.

Interview two people in the class about their shopping habits.
Place a <u>Y</u> in the box if the response is yes or an <u>N</u> in the box
if the response is no.

M F

1. Do you *shop around* before you buy something?
2. Do you ever try to *bargain* with a shopkeeper?
3. Do you buy things and then return them because
   you've changed your mind about the item?
4. Do you buy things you don't need just because they
   are on sale?
5. Do you buy things because everyone else has one?
6. Do you go shopping when you are depressed?
7. Do you usually shop at the same stores?
8. Do you watch the *infomercials* on late night TV?
9. Do you order things from a *catalogue*?
10. Do you ever buy things because of sales pressure?
11. Do you buy most things on credit?
12. Do you have more than three credit cards?
13. Do you enjoy trying on clothes?
14. Do you buy products because of the price or brand name?

Now compare the results with other students in the class.
Are the results the same for men and women?

GLOSSARY

bargain – to negotiate for a lower price

bazaar – market, sale of goods for charity

catalogue – book with items for sale usually with pictures

infomercials – program on television promoting the sale of a particular product

kayaking – boating in a closed canoe built for one person

PIN – personal identification number

RRSP – Registered Retirement Savings Plan

shop around – to go to many different stores in order to buy something at the lowest possible price

withdraw – take money out of a bank account

IDIOMS

feet are killing me – feet are very sore

hang out – to spend a lot of time in a certain place

recharge our batteries – restore our physical strength

shop 'til we drop – shop until too tired to move

UNIT 9

GOING PLACES

SETTING THE SCENE

1. What are the Lefevres doing?

2. What might they be talking about?

Chantal: Dad, when are we going to stop for lunch? I'm hungry.

Patrick: We'll stop at the next rest stop, but we're only stopping for half an hour.

Michelle: I still think we should have stopped at the last rest stop and checked the map. I have a feeling that the other route would have been faster.

Patrick: The other route might have been faster but this one is more *scenic*.

Chantal: Mom, are there any apples left?

Michelle: I'm sorry, Chantal, there aren't any left. Claude must have eaten the last one. Anyway, we're already at the rest stop.

Claude: Good. I need to *stretch my legs*.

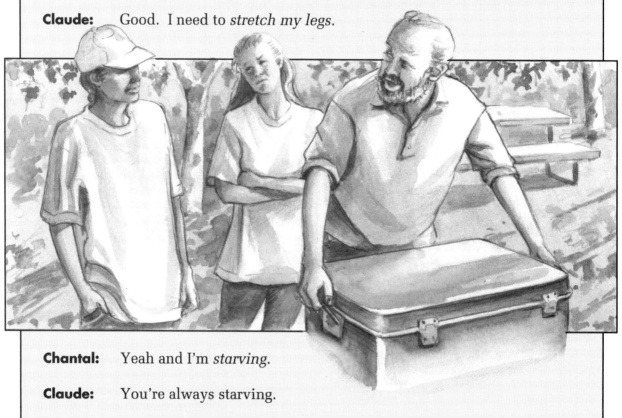

Chantal: Yeah and I'm *starving*.

Claude: You're always starving.

Chantal: That's because you're always *pigging out* and you never leave anything for anyone else.

Claude: Well, you could've had half of my apple if you had asked.

Patrick: O.K. you two stop fighting and help me take the cooler over to that picnic table.

Comprehension Check

1. Why did Michelle want to stop at the last rest stop?
2. Why did Patrick take this route?
3. Why are they stopping at the rest stop?

LET'S FOCUS

PERFECT MODALS

MUST HAVE

We use this perfect modal to make an assumption about a past action. The contraction, <u>must've</u>, is often used in spoken English.

<u>must + have + past participle</u>

E X A M P L E :　**It's six o'clock. He <u>must have left</u> by now.**

They lost their luggage.
They <u>must've been annoyed</u>.

<u>must + have + been + verb + ing</u>

E X A M P L E :　**You missed the road sign.**
You <u>must've been looking</u> at the scenery.

COULD HAVE

We use this perfect modal to express an action which the person was able to do but chose not to do; to express a possible action that did not happen; and to speculate about events in the past.

<u>could have + past participle</u>

E X A M P L E :　**He <u>could have helped</u> us push the car.**
You shouldn't have climbed over the railing.
You <u>could've broken</u> your neck!
I heard something in the woods last night.
It <u>could've been</u> a bear.

◇　**We sometimes use a negative form of the perfect modal, <u>could have</u>, to express a conviction.**

E X A M P L E :　**I just saw him. He <u>couldn't have gone</u> far.**

LET'S FOCUS

WOULD HAVE

We use this perfect modal to express the idea that we were willing to do something in the past, but did not do it.

<u>would have + past participle</u>

EXAMPLE: **You didn't ask for a ride.**
I <u>would have given</u> you a ride if you had asked me.

◇ **In <u>spoken</u> English, <u>would have</u> is often contracted in affirmative statements. In this contracted form, we don't pronounce <u>would</u>. Remember: This contraction is never used in written English.**

SHOULD HAVE

We use this perfect modal to express the feeling that an action in the past was contrary to what was expected at that time. It is frequently used to express the opinion that a possible action in the past was advisable, but not done.

<u>should + have + past participle</u>

EXAMPLE: **You <u>should have gone</u> to the Calgary Stampede while you were in Alberta.**
(You didn't go to the Calgary Stampede)

When <u>should she have arrived</u>?
(She is late)

You <u>shouldn't have driven</u> so far.
(But you did)

<u>should have been + verb + ing</u>

EXAMPLE: **You <u>should have been saving</u> your money for the trip.**
You <u>should've been looking</u> for a summer job.

◇ **Often the question form (positive and especially negative) is used to give advice or express an opinion in a very polite way.**

EXAMPLE: <u>**Shouldn't we have turned**</u> **at the last corner?**

PRACTICE 1

Complete the following sentences. Use <u>must have</u>, <u>should have</u>, <u>could have</u>, or <u>would have</u> + past participle of the verb. Use the contraction whenever possible. Use the negative form if necessary.

1. **A.** Andrea's car broke down. We were worried about her.
   B. She _____(call) us.

2. **A.** Pedro and Juanita needed a moving van on the weekend.
   B. Oh! I _____ (lend) them my truck.

3. **A.** Mahesh and Claude didn't go skiing at Mt Tremblant because they were studying for their final exams.
   B. I _____ (go) either.

4. **A.** We didn't have enough time to visit Banff and Lake Louise so we just went to Banff.
   B. You _____ (miss) Lake Louise. It's beautiful.

PRACTICE 1

5. A. Belita and Carla paid more than $600 each to fly to Vancouver.
   B. That's expensive. _____ they _____ (find) a better deal?

6. A. Pedro and Juanita went to Montreal for the June 24th weekend but they couldn't find a hotel room.
   B. _____ they _____ (made) reservations before they left?

7. A. There's Simon riding his new motorbike! Why didn't he stop?
   B. He _____n't _____ (see) us. Anyway he _____ _____ (stop). He was going too fast.

8. A. Sue and Tim took a trip to Long Beach National Park on Vancouver Island.
   B. They _____ (stay) with my sister. She lives in Tofino.

9. A. Oh, my legs are so cramped! We've been on this bus for twelve hours.
   B. Maybe we _____ (take) the train, but the bus is cheaper.

10. A. Carla took a bus from the airport when she came back from her holiday.
   B. I _____ her _____ (pick up). I work near there.

PRACTICE 2

Work together. Make up responses to the state-
ments. Use <u>must have</u>, <u>should have</u>, <u>could have</u>, or
<u>would have</u>, where appropriate.

E x a m p l e : **When we were on holiday in B.C.
we saw a black bear.**

**You <u>must have been</u> surprised.
I <u>would've fainted.</u>
The bear <u>must have been</u> afraid too.**

1. Hisako saw the Northern Lights when she visited Yellowknife.

2. Sue and Tim wanted to go whale watching when they were on
   Vancouver Island.

3. Claude hitchhiked to Calgary last summer.

4. I wanted to go camping in Algonquin Park last weekend
   but I didn't have a tent.

5. Michelle wanted to see Green Gables when they were on Prince Edward Island, but they didn't have a lot of time.

WORK TOGETHER

Pedro and Juanita took a trip to Montreal on
the June 24th weekend. They didn't realize
that this is a special holiday in Quebec—St. Jean Baptiste Day. The
city was very crowded. They were not accustomed to all the one-way
streets in Montreal and they couldn't find a hotel. Juanita usually
doesn't tell Pedro how to drive but the traffic made her so nervous
that she did a lot of *back-seat driving* on this trip.

152

WORK TOGETHER

With your partner make up some negative questions that Juanita might have asked Pedro in the following situations.

EXAMPLE: **Pedro forgot to stop at a stop sign.**
"Shouldn't you have stopped at that sign?"

1. Pedro drove by a vacancy sign on a motel.

2. Pedro turned left instead of right.

3. Pedro ran out of gas.

4. Pedro left the car running when he stopped to ask for directions.

5. Pedro spoke English when he asked for directions.

WORK TOGETHER

Sometimes we run into problems when we travel that could have been prevented. Work with a partner and talk about solutions that would have prevented the following problems.
Use should have and could have.

What would you say to someone who had:

1. lost his/her luggage
2. missed his/her flight
3. got on board the wrong train
4. lost a lot of money
5. difficulty finding accommodation
6. got seasick on a cruise
7. had difficulty communicating with the local people because he/she didn't know the language.

Now talk about problems you have encountered while travelling and ask your partner what you could have/should have done.

LET'S GET SET

1. Where are these people?

2. What are they doing?

Belita: Let's look at the *brochures*. We have information about Montreal, Toronto, Banff, and Vancouver.

Andrea: If we went to Toronto, we could go to the C.N. Tower, Ontario Place, and the Skydome. There are also lots of shows and great museums.

Steve: We could see the Blue Jays play at the Skydome.

Belita: If we went to Montreal, we could see the Olympic Stadium, the Botanical Gardens, the nightclubs, and go shopping.

Andrea: Maybe we should go to Banff and then Vancouver. If we took the train, we could just sit back, relax, and enjoy the mountain scenery.

Peter: I've always wanted to take a train ride across Canada. You know, my great great grandfather and his brothers worked on the railway.

Steve: Really, I didn't know that. It must have been backbreaking work.

Belita: I'd love to go out west by train. It would be so exciting. We could even go to the West Edmonton Mall.

Steve: If we made arrangements right away, we could go to the Calgary Stampede.

Peter: That would be great! We could see some real cowboys.

Belita: If we went to the Stampede, we'd be able to get cowboy hats.

Comprehension Check

1. What are the four friends discussing?

2. What does Belita suggest?

3. What does Andrea suggest?

4. What does Steve want to do?

LET'S FOCUS

SECOND CONDITIONAL

We use the second conditional to talk about actions that are unreal, unlikely to come true, or that we are imagining.

The verb in the <u>if</u> clause is in the simple past tense or the past continuous. The verb in the main clause takes the modals <u>would</u> or <u>could</u> and the simple form of the verb.

Sometimes the modal <u>should</u> is used, but this is not common.

Although the verb is in the past tense, we are talking about present or future possibilities. The past tense indicates that we are <u>not</u> talking about <u>real</u> situations.

E X A M P L E :   If I <u>were</u> you, I <u>would take</u> the plane. (I'm not you.)

If I <u>won</u> the lottery, I <u>would travel</u> around the world. (I don't think I will win.)

If I <u>travelled</u> across Canada by car, it <u>would take</u> at least two weeks. (I don't think I will travel by car.)

◇ In written and formal English we use just one form of the verb <u>be</u> to express an unreal condition. For all subject pronouns (I, you, we, they, he, she, it) we use <u>were.</u>

E X A M P L E :   If he <u>were</u> here, he would help us.
If I <u>were</u> rich, I would travel more often.

◇ In spoken English, the regular simple past is quite common.

E X A M P L E :   If he <u>was</u> here, he would help us.

◇ <u>Unless</u> is also used with second conditional sentences. It means <u>if not</u>.

E X A M P L E :   If I <u>didn't find</u> the ticket, I <u>wouldn't be able</u> to take the plane.
<u>Unless</u> I found the ticket, I <u>wouldn't be able</u> to take the plane.

PRACTICE 3

Peter and Simon have been planning a trip across Canada for several years. They know that it may never happen but they enjoy talking about it.

With your partner complete the following sentences using the correct form of the verbs in parentheses and an appropriate modal.

Peter: If we _____(fly) to St. John's, Newfoundland, then we _____ visit my aunt and see L'ance aux Meadows, the 1000 year old Viking settlement.

Simon: Then if we _____(have) enough money, we _____ rent a boat, see Labrador, and travel around the Gaspé Peninsula.

Peter: If we _____(get) there in the spring, it _____ be a good time to see the Beluga whales in the St. Lawrence.

Simon: I _____ visit Quebec City if I _____(have) the time.

Peter: Yes, after that we _____ have to travel to Quebec by train unless we _____ (rent) a car.

Simon: On the trip out West we _____visit Winnipeg and Regina if we_____(have) the time.

Peter: We _____ (see) them on the way back.

Simon: Gosh! Look at the time! I have to teach my judo class in 30 minutes. I _____ *forget my head if it* _____ (be, [neg.]) *attached*.

156

PRACTICE 4

Work with a partner. Think about all the places you would like to visit in Canada.

Partner A starts : "If I had a lot of money, I would visit Banff."

Partner B continues: "If I visited Banff, I would see the Rocky Mountains."

**Partner A adds
another statement :** "If I visited the Rocky Mountains, I would go skiing."

Continue for as long as you can, then choose another area of Canada and start again.

PRACTICE 5

Work with a partner. Think of all the ways to travel across Canada. Don't just think of planes, trains, and buses. Think of bicycles or hot air balloons, etc.

What would happen if you travelled by bicycle? Discuss the possibilities.

Partner A: If we travelled across Canada by bicycle, we would meet lots of people.

Partner B: If we travelled across Canada by bicycle, we would get very tired.

Work with a partner or in a small group and plan a trip to any destination in Canada.

Consider the following:

How you would get there.
What you would need to take.
What you could do once you got there.

The Calgary Stampede

Hey there all you cowboys and cowgals!

Make your reservations to the biggest western show in Canada,
the Calgary Exhibition and Stampede.

Watch as rough tough professional cowboys compete for the biggest prize money offered
at any rodeo. For ten exciting days in July see hundreds of these heroes of the west in the
following competitions:

- ◆ *bareback bronc riding* ◆ *saddle broncing* ◆ *calf roping*
- ◆ *steer wrestling* ◆ *bull riding*

Join the more than twelve million people who attend the event each year.

Watch the thrills and excitement as cowboys compete in elimination rounds leading up to a
final day of winner-take-all competition.

Don't miss the *highlight* of the exhibition, the *chuckwagon* race.

In this spectacular event four wagon teams, each pulled by four horses, race around a half-mile long
course.

Attend the livestock show featuring:

- ◆ **the International Blacksmith's Competition** ◆ **Championship auctioneers**
- ◆ *cutting horse* **competition**

Visit the old frontier western town and an authentic native village.

Two events you might see if you visit
The Calgary Stampede.

A cowboy falling off during the bull riding
competition (top).

A cowboy fighting to stay on a bucking
horse in the bareback bronc riding
competition (right).

Comprehension Check

1. If you wanted to see the Calgary Stampede when would you go
   to Calgary?
2. If you wanted to see the highlight of the exhibition, which event
   would you go to?
3. If you wanted to attend the livestock show, what would you see?

ROLE PLAY

Choose one of the following situations and make up a short role play. Work in groups of two or three.

1. A ticket agent and a customer at a bus depot.
2. At the check-in counter for an airline: Passenger is angry because the flight is overbooked.
3. You arrive at a hotel very late: The hotel has given your room away.
4. A travel agent and a customer: The customer has a limited budget.
   Try to arrange a vacation.

 FIGURE IT OUT #1

Last year Belita, Andrea, Simon, and Peter went on vacation. Each person went to a different place and each used a different means of transportation.

Use the following clues to match the vacationer to his/her destination and means of transportation. The four destinations were Ottawa, Toronto, Vancouver, and Montreal. The four means of transportation were bus, car, train, and plane.

1. Peter who is afraid of flying did not go to Montreal.
2. Simon visited friends in the Capital.
3. Andrea drove to her destination.
4. Belita looked down on the mountains with admiration as she travelled to her destination.
5. Simon chatted with people in the dining car during the trip.
6. The person who went to Vancouver does not have a driver's licence.
7. Belita was not the one who took the bus to Toronto.

	Destination	**Transportation**
Belita		
Andrea		
Peter		
Simon		

FIGURE IT OUT #2

To solve this puzzle, determine whether the following statements are true or false. If the statement is true, write the first letter, shown in the brackets at the end of each statement, in the space below. If the answer is false, write the second letter.

1. If it were 1 p.m. in Toronto, it would be 10 a.m in Vancouver. (N/O)

2. The Klondike Gold Rush was in the Northwest Territories. (R/U)

3. The Prairies include the provinces of British Columbia, Alberta, and Saskatchewan. (P/N)

4. More than three-quarters of all Canadian manufactured goods are produced in Ontario and Quebec. (A/L)

5. Canada's regions are the West Coast, the Prairies, Central Canada, the Maritimes, and the Territories. (V/M)

6. Banff is in the province of Manitoba. (B/E)

7. The native inhabitants of Canada's most northern regions are called the Inuit. (T/D)

8. Niagara Falls is shaped like a horseshoe. (N/R)

9. The smallest province in Canada is Nova Scotia. (P/W)

10. Toronto means the "meeting place." (T/Q)

In 1999 ⃝⃝⃝⃝⃝⃝ will become Canada's newest territory.
It is the eastern part of the ⃝⃝⃝.

GLOSSARY

auctioneer – person who sells by auction (i.e., to the highest bidder)

bareback bronc riding – a competition in which a cowboy tries to stay on the back of a bucking horse which is wearing only a rope belt around its middle. He may hold onto the rope with only one hand

blacksmith – a person who works with iron (e.g., makes horseshoes)

brochures – a booklet or pamphlet with information

bull riding – a competition in which a cowboy tries to ride a bull for a timed period

calf roping – a timed competition in which a mounted cowboy chases a calf, lassoes it, dismounts, throws the calf to the ground, and ties up three of its feet with a short rope

chuckwagon – the wagon that carried food supplies on a cattle drive (when the cattle walked long distances to market)

cutting horses – saddle horses trained for use in separating an individual cow, etc. from a herd

highlight – main or most important event

saddle broncing – event in which a cowboy tries to stay in the saddle on the back of a bucking horse

scenic – having a nice view

steer wrestling – event in which a cowboy grabs a steer by the horns and tries to force it down on the ground

IDIOMS

back-seat driving – when a person who is not driving tells the person who is driving how to drive

pig out – to eat a lot

starving – very hungry

stretch my legs – to relieve the cramped feeling after sitting in a car seat for a long time

to forget one's head if it wasn't attached – to be very forgetful

ANSWERS TO FIGURE IT OUT #1

Belita	Vancouver	plane
Andrea	Montreal	car
Peter	Toronto	bus
Simon	Ottawa	train

ANSWERS TO FIGURE IT OUT #2

N U N A V E T, N W T

UNIT 10

TAKING PART

SETTING THE SCENE

1. What do you think Juanita and Michelle might be talking about?

2. Why are they standing outside a government office?

Juanita: I just saw Paul. He didn't even say "Hi."

Michelle: He's been *down in the dumps* since he took the citizenship exam. He hadn't studied and so he failed.

Juanita: He should've taken the course that I took. I had never bothered to learn anything about Canadian history, laws, or government before I took the course. Now I bet I know more than the average Canadian.

Michelle: When I told him that he should take a course he laughed and said that he didn't need to. He said that the test would be a *piece of cake*. But a couple of days before the exam he went to the library and got some books.

Juanita: Why?

Michelle: He suddenly realized that the exam might not be so easy. So he spent the last two days *cramming*. But it didn't help.

Juanita: Well he'd better register for a course if he wants to pass the exam.

Michelle: Were the questions very difficult?

Juanita: Not really. The course really prepared me well for the exam.

Michelle: I probably would've been too nervous to answer the judge's questions.

Juanita: I was really nervous just before I saw the judge. But when I went in, the judge was so reassuring that I relaxed.

Michelle: Well congratulations on becoming a Canadian citizen.

Juanita: Thanks. Pedro and I are *going out on the town* to celebrate tonight.

Comprehension Check

1. What is wrong with Paul?
2. What does Juanita suggest that Paul should have done?
3. Why didn't Paul take a citizenship course?
4. Was the citizenship course useful to Juanita?

LET'S FOCUS

PAST PERFECT

The past perfect is often used with the simple past to indicate an action that comes before another past action. It is used in the following ways:

1. in spoken and written English when the sequence of actions is very important.
2. when the verb in the simple past is not expressed but understood from the context.

had + past participle

E X A M P L E :   John <u>had</u> already <u>left</u>.
<u>Had</u> John already <u>left</u> when you arrived?
We <u>hadn't</u> <u>planned</u> to stay in Ottawa but the city was so interesting that we did.
John and Mary were really excited about their trip to Spain. They <u>had picked up</u> their tickets and passports weeks before they left.

We often use adverbs of time such as <u>before</u>, <u>after</u>, and <u>when</u> with this structure. Often, in spoken English, only the simple past is used with adverbs of time.

E X A M P L E :   The plane <u>left</u> before I <u>got</u> to the departure gate.

LET'S FOCUS

PAST PERFECT CONTINUOUS

We use the past perfect continuous when we want to emphasize the continuous nature of the action.

had been + verb + ing

E X A M P L E :   I <u>had been driving</u> for several days in order to get home in time for Christmas.

166

PRACTICE 1

Complete the following sentences. Use the past perfect or the past perfect continuous and the simple past.

E X A M P L E :   Toronto **had been** (be) a French fur-trading post before John Graves Simcoe **chose** it for the capital of Upper Canada in 1794.

1. Native Peoples _____ (live) in Canada for several thousand years before the Vikings _____ (arrive).

2. The Vikings _____ (sail) from Norway to Iceland and then to Greenland before they _____ (land) in Newfoundland.

3. The Native Peoples _____ (establish) many trading partnerships before the Europeans _____ (make) their way up the St. Lawrence.

4. After the Europeans _____ (settle) in Canada, the Native Peoples _____ (catch) many diseases that had been previously unknown.

5. The French from Quebec _____ (explore) much of Canada before the British _____ (arrive).

6. They _____ (establish) a series of fur-trading posts along the Great Lakes.

7. Port Royal in Nova Scotia _____ also _____ (be) a French settlement before it _____ (become) a British fort.

8. Quebec and Ontario _____ (be) one territory before the British ____ (divide) it.

9. The capital of Ontario _____ originally _____ (be) Niagara-on-the-Lake, but Simcoe _____ (feel) it was too close to the American border.

PRACTICE 2

Here are a list of events in Canadian history. With your partner put the events together using the past perfect and the simple past to indicate the time sequence. You can leave out the dates.

EXAMPLE:

Native People 30,000 BC   (live)   Vikings 1000 AD

The Native Peoples had lived in Canada long before the Vikings arrived.

1. Vikings 1000 AD   (arrive)   Christopher Columbus 1492

2. The French, Quebec City   (settle)   Montreal 1642
   1608

3. Capital of Upper Canada, (to be)   Capital of Upper Canada,
   after 1794: York   before 1794:
                                        Niagara-on-the-Lake

4. British, Washington 1814 (burn)   Americans attacked York 1813

5. Sir John A. MacDonald   (build)   British Columbia joined
   railway 1885   the Confederation 1886

PRACTICE 3

Work together. Talk about your own personal history. Draw a time line of the important events in your life.

Then talk about your life with a partner.

EXAMPLE:

X————————X————————X————————X————————X
born   studied   became   got married   moved
            medicine   a doctor   to Canada

EXAMPLE: If I hadn't studied medicine, I wouldn't have become a doctor.

LET'S GET SET

1. Where are Pedro and Patrick?

2. What are they talking about?

A NEW CANADIAN

Patrick: Congratulations Pedro! Michelle told me that you and Juanita passed your citizenship exams.

Pedro: Thanks. We're both really happy.

Patrick: You'll be able to vote in the elections now.

Pedro: If we had taken our tests earlier, we could have voted in the last election.

Patrick: A lot of people don't bother to vote in provincial elections.

Pedro: Well I think they're making a big mistake. It's our responsibility as citizens to vote in all the elections whether they're municipal, provincial, or federal.

Patrick: I agree. But a lot of people *take* their rights and responsibilities *for granted*.

Pedro: If they had ever lived in a country where they couldn't vote or where the elections are *rigged*, they would realize how lucky they are.

Patrick: You're right. Who would you have voted for if you could have voted?

Pedro: I probably would have voted for the *incumbent*.

Comprehension Check

1. Why is Patrick congratulating Pedro?

2. What could Pedro do now that he couldn't do before?

3. What does Pedro believe is every citizen's responsibility?

4. What are the three levels of government?

LET'S FOCUS

THIRD CONDITIONAL

We use the third conditional to talk about past actions that were possible but did not happen.

The verb in the <u>if</u> clause is in the past perfect or the past perfect continuous tense.

The main clause takes <u>would have</u>, <u>should have</u>, <u>might have</u>, or <u>could have</u> + <u>past participle form</u> of the verb.

> E X A M P L E :   **If I <u>had won</u> the lottery, I <u>would have quit</u> my job.**
> **(I did not win the lottery and I did not quit my job.)**
>
> **If she <u>hadn't lost</u> her wallet, she <u>would've bought</u> the tickets.**
> **(She lost her wallet and she didn't buy the tickets.)**

PRACTICE 4

Complete the following sentences.
Use the third conditional.

> E X A M P L E :   **If the United States <u>hadn't won</u> the American Revolution, many United Empire Loyalists <u>would</u> not <u>have come</u> (come) to Canada.**

1. If Laura Secord _____ not _____ (warn) the British of the American attack, they _____ (lost) the battle.

2. If William Lyon Mackenzie _____ not _____ (emigrate) from Scotland, he _____ not _____ (lead) the rebellion in 1837.

3. If William Lyon Mackenzie _____ not _____ (lead) the rebellion in 1837, Ontario _____ not _____ (get) a representative government.

Here are some scenes and portraits from Canadian history.

The official ceremony to drive the last spike to complete the railroad (top).

Sir John A. Macdonald in 1856 (right).

Louis Riel (middle).

Workers laying track for the railroad (bottom).

PRACTICE 4

4. If Sir John A. Macdonald _____ not _____ (be) able to send soldiers to Manitoba on the train, Louis Riel _____ (win) the rebellion.

5. If Riel _____ (win) the rebellion, the British _____ not _____ (hang) him.

6. If Macdonald _____ not _____ (complete) the railroad, British Columbia _____ not _____ (join) Confederation. It _____ (become) part of the United States.

PRACTICE 5

Here is the story of two young people living in the city of York in 1812.

Paul was a servant in a rich man's house. He fell in love with Helena, the daughter of the family. Because Paul was very poor, Helena's father refused to let her marry him. Paul asked Helena to run away with him to America, but she refused. Instead, Helena married a rich man chosen for her by her father. She was very unhappy. Paul joined the army and because he was very brave he became a captain. After the war he was able to start his own business and he became very rich. Helena was always very unhappy because she didn't marry Paul.

With a partner, tell how things could have been different for Paul and Helena.

E X A M P L E :   **If Paul <u>had been</u> rich, he <u>could have married</u> Helena.**

WORK TOGETHER

Many inventions and discoveries were made by chance. Can you think of some things that might be different today if they hadn't been made?

E X A M P L E :   **If Columbus hadn't got lost, he wouldn't have discovered North America.**

If the automobile hadn't been invented, we might still be using horses for transportation.

LET'S FOCUS

INDIRECT SPEECH 2

(Review the rules for indirect speech in Unit 4.)

When we change direct speech to indirect speech, verbs in the present perfect or the simple past tense change to the past perfect tense.

E X A M P L E :   **"I have never visited Niagara Falls," said Mary.**
Mary said (that) she had never visited Niagara Falls.
"We went last week," said Paul.
Paul said they had gone last week.

Often in spoken English we do not change the simple past to the past perfect. We leave it in the simple past tense.

E X A M P L E :   **Paul said, "We took my in-laws to see the Falls."**
Paul said that they took his in-laws to see the Falls.

DIRECT SPEECH	INDIRECT SPEECH
Present Perfect ———————>	Past Perfect
Present Perfect Continuous ——>	Past Perfect Continuous
Simple Past ————————>	Past Perfect
Past Continuous ——————>	Past Perfect Continuous

◇ **In general, modals such as <u>would</u>, <u>should</u>, <u>could</u>, and <u>might</u> remain unchanged.**

◇ **Pronouns change from 1st person to 3rd person in indirect speech.**

PRACTICE 6

Change the following quotations to indirect speech.

1. The American General said, "We fought hard, but we lost."

2. General Brock said, "We have burnt Washington."

3. My great grandmother told me, "It took three weeks to sail from Ireland to Canada and I was seasick all the way."

4. My mother told me, "My family came from Germany before they settled in Kitchener."

5. My father said, "I think your grandparents came from Ukraine around *the turn of the century*."

6. The pioneers complained, "We have been working hard to clear this land but it has been very difficult."

7. The teacher said, "Children should be seen and not heard."

8. The Mennonites said, "We came to Canada to find religious freedom."

PRACTICE 7

◇ **Below are two letters; one from an early settler and one from his wife. One student should read Harry's letter, the other should read Sarah's letter, then tell each other what the letters said.**

Dear Sarah,

We arrived at Halifax last month. The voyage took three long weeks and many people died of smallpox on the way. Your brother John was sick but recovered.

We left Halifax as soon as we were able and travelled by stage to York where John and I bought some land. We have been clearing the land and building a small cabin.

I wanted to send money for your passage but we wouldn't have enough to buy food if I did that. You should be patient.

Your husband,
Harry

PRACTICE 7

Dear Harry,

We have not yet received a letter from you and John. The three children have been sick and since the potato crop failed there has not been enough food for them.

My father lent me enough money to pay our passage and I have decided to leave Ireland and join you in Halifax.

Your wife,
Sarah

LET'S FOCUS

PAST PERFECT AND INDIRECT SPEECH: QUESTION FORMATION

Yes/No Questions

When putting yes/no questions into indirect speech, introduce the subordinate clause with <u>if</u> and change the question form to a statement. No question mark is necessary.

E X A M P L E :   **He asked, "Did you live in Quebec for a while?"**
He asked if I had lived in Quebec for a while.

◇ <u>**Whether**</u> **is an alternative for** <u>**if.**</u>

Information Questions

When changing information questions into <u>indirect speech</u>, introduce the subordinate clause with the appropriate question word and change the question form to a statement. No question mark is necessary.

E X A M P L E :   **She asked, "Where did you go after you left Montreal?"**
She asked where I had gone after I left Montreal.

PRACTICE 8

Change the following questions to indirect speech.

The Centennial celebrations on Parliament Hill.

EXAMPLE: **"Did you have a good time?" she asked.**
She asked if I had had a good time.

1. "How long have you been studying Canadian history?" Meena asked.

2. "Were you able to pass your citizenship exam?" he wanted to know.

3. "When did Canada become a nation?" she wondered.

4. "When did Newfoundland join Confederation?" they asked.

5. "Who was the first Prime Minister of Canada?" the judge asked.

6. "Why was Ottawa chosen as the capital of Canada?" the boy asked.

7. "Who was the first woman Governor General of Canada?" she asked.

8. "Did many people come from the United States after the American Revolution?" he asked.

9. "When was the Charter of Rights and Freedoms written?" they inquired.

10. "What did the word "Canada" mean originally?" she asked.

CANADIAN CHARTER OF RIGHTS AND FREEDOMS

The Canadian Charter of Rights and Freedoms was added to the Canadian Constitution in 1982. The Charter guarantees some fundamental freedoms and rights to all citizens. The following is a condensed version of the charter.

Fundamental Freedoms
This ensures all citizens freedom of religion, thought, belief, expression, association, and the press.

Democratic Rights
This allows all citizens the right to vote or actively participate in elections.

Mobility Rights
All citizens have the right to enter, remain in, and leave Canada. It also permits citizens to move from one province to another. They may also pursue a livelihood in any province.

Legal Rights
Everyone has the right:
- to life, liberty, and security of the person.
- to be secure against unreasonable search or seizure.
- to not be *arbitrarily* detained or imprisoned.
- upon detention to be informed *promptly* of the reasons for detention and to be informed of their right to retain and instruct *counsel* without delay.

Equality Rights
Guarantees that every individual is equal before and under the law without discrimination; in particular discrimination based on race, national or ethnic origin, colour, religion, sex, age, or mental or physical disability.

Official Languages
English and French are the official languages of Canada and have equality of status and equal rights and privileges as to their use in all institutions of the Parliament and government of Canada and of New Brunswick.

Minority Language Educational Rights
Canadians belonging to a minority group of speakers of either English or French in their province may have their children educated in the language of the minority, where numbers warrant the creation of minority language schools.

Enforcement
Any citizen who feels his/her rights as guaranteed in this charter have been violated may apply to the courts to obtain a remedy.

General
The rights and freedoms expressed in the Charter apply to men and women equally.

Comprehension Check

1. What is the Charter of Rights and Freedoms?

2. When was the Charter of Rights and Freedoms added to the Canadian Constitution?

3. What rights does it guarantee citizens who wish to move from one province to another?

4. What are some of the legal rights guaranteed in the Charter?

5. What are the fundamental freedoms guaranteed in the Charter?

WORK TOGETHER

You and your partner(s) belong to a political party.
Draft your own charter of rights. What would you include and why?

GLOSSARY

arbitrarily – without a legitimate reason
counsel – legal or official advice
incumbent – person who is presently in power at a particular level of government
mobility – able to move freely
promptly – in a short amount of time
turn of the century – at the beginning of a new century

IDIOMS

down in the dumps – depressed
cram – to study as much as possible at the last minute
go out on the town – to go out for an evening
piece of cake – easy
rigged – arranged dishonestly
take for granted – to accept without appreciation

UNIT

11 REASONS TO CELEBRATE

SETTING THE SCENE

1. What are Andrea and her friends planning to do?

Andrea: We're out of milk, I'll buy some as soon as the stores open tomorrow.

Belita: It's Canada Day. All the banks, shops, and businesses will be closed.

Andrea: Of course. I forgot. I promised I'd take my little cousins to see the parade and the fireworks tomorrow.

Meena: Where are the fireworks displays being held?

Andrea: There will be fireworks displays in most community parks.

Belita: It's interesting that in most cultures holidays are celebrated with parades and fireworks.

Meena: You're right. One of the biggest festivals for Hindus is Diwali and it's always celebrated with fireworks.

Peter: There's always a parade for Chinese New Year.

Simon: We're lucky because in Canada each of the various ethnic groups is encouraged to maintain its cultural identity and religion.

Peter: I've learned a lot from attending the festivals of various cultures.

Simon: So have I. Why don't we all go to see the parade and the fireworks tomorrow.

Comprehension Check

1. What has Andrea promised to do on Canada Day?

2. What other two holidays are mentioned?

3. What does Simon suggest?

LET'S FOCUS

PASSIVE VOICE

Usually we use the active voice. In this voice the subject of the sentence performs the action.

E X A M P L E :   <u>We gave</u> **Peter a surprise party for his 21st birthday.**

Sometimes the most important person or thing in the sentence does not do anything. In these cases we use the passive voice. We form the passive voice by using the appropriate form of the verb <u>be</u> and the <u>past participle</u> of the verb.

E X A M P L E :   **Peter <u>was surprised</u> by the party.**
Canada Day <u>is celebrated</u> on July 1st.

◇ **Most tenses that exist in the active voice also exist in the passive voice. The perfect continuous forms, however, are extremely rare in the passive voice.**

E X A M P L E :

Active	Passive
Simple Present:	
Mary <u>bakes</u> a cake.	The cake <u>is baked</u> by Mary.
Present Continuous:	
Mary <u>is baking</u> a cake.	The cake <u>is being baked</u> by Mary.
Simple Past:	
Mary <u>baked</u> a cake.	The cake <u>was baked</u> by Mary.
Past Continuous:	
Mary <u>was baking</u> a cake.	The cake <u>was being baked</u> by Mary.
Present Perfect:	
Mary <u>has baked</u> a cake.	The cake <u>has been baked</u> by Mary.
Past Perfect:	
Mary <u>had baked</u> a cake.	The cake <u>had been baked</u> by Mary.
Future:	
Mary <u>will bake a cake</u>.	The cake <u>will be baked</u> by Mary.
Mary <u>is going to bake</u> a cake.	The cake <u>is going to be baked</u> by Mary.
Modals:	
Mary <u>can bake</u> a cake.	The cake <u>can be baked</u> by Mary.

182

LET'S FOCUS

◇ **When we use the passive voice and we want to include the person who performed the action, we use the preposition by + agent. By + agent is not always necessary.**

   E X A M P L E :   The party was given <u>by Peter's friends</u>.
   Christmas is celebrated in many different ways.

◇ **The passive voice can be used to avoid overly wordy or awkward sentences, but do not overuse the passive voice.**

   E X A M P L E :   awkward: Someone sent the invitations last week.
   better: The invitations were sent last week.

PRACTICE 1

Rewrite the following sentences using the <u>passive voice</u>. Do not use <u>by + agent</u> unless you feel it is important. Make sure your new subject agrees with the verb.

   E X A M P L E :   **People celebrate the Chinese New Year in January or February.**
   The Chinese New Year <u>is celebrated</u> in January or February.

1. People commemorate the Day of the Dead on November 1 in Mexico.

2. People have celebrated Christmas in December for almost 2000 years.

3. Before that, Celtic people marked the Winter Solstice on December 21.

4. Romans celebrated the Festival of Saturnalia at this time.

5. Some Iranians observe Nourooz (New Year) on March 21.

PRACTICE 2

Look at the following sentences. Some of these sentences should be changed to the passive. Work with a partner and decide which sentences to change and then write down the new sentences.

1. My mother bore me on May 4, 1960.

2. I graduated from university in 1982.

3. I married my husband in 1983.

4. His family sponsored us to come to Canada the next year.

5. It took a long time but finally someone sent us our immigration papers.

6. We worked hard to make a new life here.

7. I bore my first child in 1989.

8. I decided to take the TOEFL test but I didn't have much time.

9. People had to write the test on a certain date.

10. I got a good mark and now I can go back to school.

PRACTICE 3

Many different holidays are celebrated around the world. When people come to Canada they bring their traditions with them. Talk about a special holiday you celebrate. Try to use the passive voice where appropriate.

EXAMPLE: **Passover <u>is celebrated</u> in the spring.**
             Special <u>foods are eaten</u> at this time.

LET'S GET SET

1. Where do you think these people are?

2. What are they doing?

Patrick: Come in. Michelle and I are happy about having you here this evening to help us celebrate.

Sunil: Thank you for inviting us.

Patrick: Let's go into the family room.

Monica: This is a beautiful home, Michelle.

Michelle: Thank you. I'm thrilled about finally having a house big enough to entertain all our friends at once.

Belita: This is a great housewarming party, isn't it? Do you think we'll ever be able to afford a house like this?

Peter: Maybe one day. Right now I'm worried about paying the rent.

Belita: Well when we get married we'll have to economize.

Carla: Did I hear you say you were getting married?

Belita: I was going to tell you when we got home. Peter proposed this afternoon.

Carla: Congratulations, you two. I know you'll both be very happy. I can't wait to tell Andrea and Meena. They'll be delighted at the news.

LATER . . .

Ting Mei: I'm sorry we have to leave so soon. But Sue Yen isn't feeling well.

Michelle: I'm sorry to hear you're not feeling well Sue Yen, but I'm glad you both came.

Sue Yen: We had a very nice time. Thanks for inviting us.

Ting Mei: Yes, thank you for a very pleasant evening. We hope you'll be very happy in your new home.

Comprehension Check

1. Where are the people in the dialogue?

2. Why is Carla congratulating Belita and Peter?

3. Why are Ting Mei and Sue Yen leaving early?

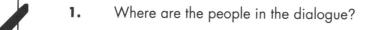

◇ LET'S FOCUS

USED TO and WOULD

Used to and would are used to talk about past actions which are not performed any longer.

E X A M P L E :   **Past Habit:**
I <u>used to smoke</u>. (but I don't smoke now)

Past Condition:
He <u>used to be</u> fat. (but now he's thin)

Regular repeated actions:
We <u>used to go</u> to my grandmother's house for the holidays.
My grandmother <u>would</u> bake delicious cookies for us.

◇ **<u>Would</u> is only used for regularly repeated actions; not for past habits or situations.**

PRACTICE 4

Fill in the blanks with <u>would</u> or <u>used to</u>.

E X A M P L E :   **I <u>used to</u> bite my nails.**

1. I _____ speak French at home.

2. My father _____ take us for long walks.

3. My mother _____ tell me bedtime stories.

4. My brother _____ stutter.

5. I didn't _____ smoke.

6. Did you _____ believe in Santa Claus?

7. We _____ save our money to buy presents.

8. My mother _____ bake a delicious pumpkin pie at Thanksgiving.

9. My sister _____ live far away but she _____ always come home for Passover.

10. My grandfather _____ sing beautiful songs in his language and then he and my uncles _____ dance.

PRACTICE 5

Fill in the blanks with <u>used to</u> and <u>would</u>. Use <u>used to</u> for old habits or situations. Use <u>would</u> for repeated actions.

E X A M P L E :   **When I was young, my father <u>would</u> give me rides on his back.**

PRACTICE 5

When I was young, we _____ live in a big house with my grandparents and my aunts, uncles, and cousins. Every summer my grandfather _____ take my cousins and me to the seaside while our parents stayed at home to work. We_____ take a train across the mountains to the sea. We _____ get very excited when we saw the sea. My grandfather _____ smoke a pipe in the house and my grandmother _____ always make him go outside. I _____ be a good swimmer and enjoyed swimming in the waves but my grandparents _____ worry about me. After our summer vacation my grandparents took us back home. Our parents _____ come to meet us at the station. We were glad to see them but we _____ miss the seaside.

WORK TOGETHER

With a partner write down questions about what people did as children. Find another pair of students and interview them. Then answer their questions.

E X A M P L E : **When you were a child <u>did you use</u> to eat all your vegetables?**
When you were a child <u>would you</u> play tricks on people?

LET'S FOCUS

PAST PARTICIPLES AS ADJECTIVES

Very often we use the past participles of regular verbs to talk about emotions. These past participles are used as adjectives. The past participle describes how a person feels or is affected by something.

E X A M P L E : **I am amaz<u>ed</u>!**

LET'S FOCUS

Here is a list of some common past participle adjectives and their prepositions.

LIST

afraid of	frightened by	surprised by
amused by	interested in	terrified of
annoyed with	pleased with	thrilled with
ashamed of	scared of	tired of
bored with	shocked by (at)	worried about
excited by		

◇ **This type of adjective form is often used with verbs such as <u>be</u>, <u>feel</u>, <u>seem</u>, <u>look</u>, and <u>appear</u>.**

E X A M P L E :   **She <u>seemed amused</u> by the clown.**

When these past participles are completed by another verb, the form is <u>adjective</u> + <u>preposition</u> + <u>gerund</u>.

E X A M P L E :   **I am <u>interested in watching</u> basketball games.**

LET'S FOCUS

PRESENT PARTICIPLES AS ADJECTIVES

We also use the present participle or gerund form as an adjective.
The <u>ing</u> form describes the effect of a person or a thing on others.

E X A M P L E :   **She was <u>amusing</u>.**
                        Planning a wedding is <u>tiring</u>.

PRACTICE 6

Fill in the blanks with the appropriate preposition.

EXAMPLE: **She was amused <u>by</u> the singing.**

1. They were bored _____ playing games at the party.

2. Andrew felt ashamed _____ his old clothes when he first came to Canada.

3. We were interested _____ the lecture on immigrant contributions to Canada.

4. Belita appeared surprised _____ her present.

5. Pedro was worried _____ passing his citizenship exam.

6. Ting Mei and Sue Yen are excited _____ the birth of their baby.

7. Mr. and Mrs. Sharma are surprised _____ many things in Canada.

8. They were shocked _____ the cost of renting an apartment.

9. Meena was frightened _____ writing her final exams.

10. Michelle and Patrick felt thrilled _____ buying a new house.

PRACTICE 7

Choose the correct form of the adjectives in parentheses. Use the correct preposition where necessary.

EXAMPLE: **She is an <u>interesting</u> person. (interest)**
              She is <u>interested in</u> archeology. (interest)

1. Dancing can be _____. (tire)

PRACTICE 7

2. She was _____ the jack o'lanterns at Halloween. (scare)

3. They were _____ their Lucky Money which their grandparents gave them. (thrill)

4. Children are always _____ Santa Claus. (excite)

5. I find too many parties _____. (bore)

6. Sue Yen was _____ the baby shower. (surprise)

7. The TOEFL exam was _____ but I got 600 anyway. (terrify)

8. Different customs are always _____ . (interest)

9. Our neighbours were _____ the noise at our party so we invited them over. (annoy)

10. Sue Yen was _____ the presents for her baby. (please)

PRACTICE 8

With your partner make a list of things that please, excite, shock, or annoy you about living in Canada.

EXAMPLE: **I am pleased with the Health Care system.**

PRACTICE 9

Complete the following dialogue between Simon and Andrea and find out what Simon is shocked about. Supply the missing preposition.

Simon: Andrea, have you seen Meena? She was interested _____ looking at some used cars.

Andrea: She's gone over to her parents' house. They want her to meet a *matchmaker.* She was a little nervous _____ going. They're arranging a marriage for her.

Simon: An arranged marriage? They can't do that!

Andrea: Why not? It's part of their culture and they're not forcing her into anything.

Simon: Well I'm going to talk to her. I can't believe she's thinking_____ marrying a stranger.

Andrea: Leave her alone Simon. She'll be angry _____ my telling you. She's only going to meet the matchmaker. If he finds a suitable match, he'll introduce them and then it's up to them.

ROLE PLAY

Simon is very upset that Meena may be getting married to a stranger. Work with a partner and take the parts of Simon and Meena.

As Simon, try to convince Meena that she might be making a big mistake.

As Meena, try to explain to Simon why she is considering an arranged marriage.

Building a Nation

All the various cultural groups living in Canada have had a significant impact on its growth. Most came hoping to make a better life for themselves. In the process they have helped to build a nation. In the early days of *nationhood* they came and worked as labourers on the railroad, as farmers in the fields, and skilled and unskilled workers in factories. In more recent times new Canadians have invested in businesses. One group of Canadians who managed to overcome great *hardship* and achieve success in Canada are the Canadians of Chinese ancestry.

The Chinese first came to Canada in the 1800's. After the *gold rush* in California ended they went to British Columbia. They came as miners attracted by the rich *mineral deposits*. Soon many were recruited as labourers in the railway gangs that built the Canadian Pacific Railroad. They were poorly paid and many died because of the dangerous working conditions. After the completion of the railroad many Chinese left Canada while others remained and worked in factories, private homes, or started their own businesses. Today's Chinese-Canadians have become successful in business and have entered other professions such as law, medicine, and politics.

Comprehension Check

1. What were the occupations of the early immigrants to Canada?

2. When did the Chinese first come to Canada?

3. What did most of them end up doing?

4. What did the Chinese do after the railroad was completed?

 WORK TOGETHER

In small groups discuss current and past contributions of one of Canada's ethnic communities. Write a report and present it to the rest of the class.

DISCUSS ◆◆◆◆◆◆◆◆◆◆◆◆◆◆◆◆◆◆◆◆◆◆◆

What are some of the challenges that face new Canadians?
What advice would you give them?

WORK TOGETHER

In small groups plan a party. Decide the following together:

a. the reason for the party

b. the guest list

c. the refreshments

d. the entertainment.

FIGURE IT OUT

Do you know the name of the holiday described?
What date is this holiday?
Complete the following with the appropriate verb
in the passive voice and the name of the holiday.

1. Green beer _____ (serve) in pubs on _____.

2. Candy _____ (give) to trick or treaters on _____.

3. Practical jokes _____ (play) on _____.

4. Eggs _____ (decorate) and _____ (hide) at _____.

5. Pumpkin pie _____ (eat) for dessert on _____.

6. Poppies _____ (wear) on _____.

7. Children _____ (photograph) with a jolly fat man in a red suit at _____.

8. "Auld Lang Syne" _____ (sing) at midnight on _____.

9. On _____ an animal _____(watch) as he comes out of his burrow. If he sees his own shadow, there will be six more weeks of winter.

10. Fireworks _____(set off) to celebrate a Queen's birthday on _____.

GLOSSARY

archeology – study of ancient artifacts and objects

gold rush – historical era in which gold and other minerals were being discovered in the Klondike, leading to rapid economic growth

hardship – difficult circumstances

matchmaker – a person who arranges for single people to meet each other

mineral deposits – geological location of minerals

nationhood – status or identity as a nation

ANSWERS TO FIGURE IT OUT

1. St. Patrick's Day
2. Halloween
3. April Fool's Day
4. Easter

5. Thanksgiving
6. Remembrance Day
7. Christmas

8. New Year's Eve
9. Ground Hog Day
10. Victoria Day

List of Irregular Verbs

1 Verbs which are the same in all three forms

Root Form	Simple Past	Past Participle
cost	cost	cost
cut	cut	cut
hit	hit	hit
hurt	hurt	hurt
let	let	let
put	put	put
set	set	set
shut	shut	shut

2 Verbs which have the same form for **simple past** and **past** participle

Root Form	Simple Past	Past Participle
bend	bent	bent
bring	brought	brought
build	built	built
burn	burned/burnt	burned/burnt
buy	bought	bought
catch	caught	caught
dig	dug	dug
dream	dreamed/dreamt	dreamed/dreamt
feed	fed	fed
feel	felt	felt
find	found	found
get	got	got
have	had	had
hear	heard	heard
hold	held	held
keep	kept	kept
lay	laid	laid
learn	learned/learnt	learned/learnt
leave	left	left
lend	lent	lent
lose	lost	lost
make	made	made
mean	meant	meant

List of Irregular Verbs *Continued*

Root Form	Simple Past	Past Principle
meet	met	met
read	read	read
say	said	said
sell	sold	sold
send	sent	sent
shine	shone	shone
shoot	shot	shot
sit	sat	sat
sleep	slept	slept
slide	slid	slid
smell	smelled/smelt	smelled/smelt
spell	spelled/spelt	spelled/spelt
spend	spent	spent
stand	stood	stood
teach	taught	taught
tell	told	told
think	thought	thought
understand	understood	understood
win	won	won

3 Verbs which have the same form for the **root form** and the **past participle**

Root Form	Simple Past	Past Participle
become	became	become
come	came	come
run	ran	run

4 One Verb has the same form for the **root form** and the **simple past**

Root form	Simple Past	Past Participle
beat	beat	beaten

5 Verbs which are different in all three forms

Root Form	Simple Past	Past Participle
be	was	been
begin	began	begun
bite	bit	bitten
blow	blew	blown
break	broke	broken
choose	chose	chosen
do	did	done
draw	drew	drawn
drink	drank	drunk
drive	drove	driven
eat	ate	eaten
fall	fell	fallen
fly	flew	flown
forget	forgot	forgotten
freeze	froze	frozen
give	gave	given
go	went	gone
hide	hid	hidden
know	knew	known
lie	lay	lain
ride	rode	ridden
ring	rang	rung
see	saw	seen
shake	shook	shaken
sing	sang	sung
speak	spoke	spoken
steal	stole	stolen
swim	swam	swum
take	took	taken
tear	tore	torn
throw	threw	thrown
wear	wore	worn
write	wrote	written